The New English Grammar

Charles Lamar Thompson, Ed.D.

Associate Professor of English Education
Memphis State University

Lear Siegler, Inc./Fearon Publishers
Belmont, California

This book is affectionately dedicated to Ford Haynes, Jr., Chairman of the Department of Secondary Education, Memphis State University, and Heber Rumble, former Chairman of the Department of Secondary Education, Memphis State University, for making it possible for me to "grow on the job."

ISBN-0-8224-4650-2

Library of Congress Catalog Card Number: 74-88785

Printed in the United States of America.

Contents

Preface

The "new" English grammar is a blending of four systems of grammar: traditional, historical, structural, and transformational. This book is distinguished by the fact that these four approaches to grammar have been fused in a logical and practical style. Traditional grammar provides most of the terminology; historical grammar provides the historical background; structural grammar provides the sentence patterns; transformational grammar provides the variations of the sentence patterns.

Traditional grammar, often called "prescriptive grammar," has its roots in classical Latin. Adopted by eighteenth-century grammarians, traditional grammar has eight parts of speech, twelve verb tenses, and Latin-derived concepts and terminology. It was assumed that Latin was the most logical of all languages and that its grammar should provide the terminology, definitions, rules, and models for teaching English. Without being questioned, this Latin system has been used in our schools for two hundred years. Most English teachers today know the system thoroughly and feel very comfortable with it, although an increasing number are becoming disenchanted with it because of its many inconsistencies and a growing feeling of its inadequacy.

Historical grammar gives us the history of English and its relationships with other languages of the world. Otto Jespersen, a

V

Danish scholar, is the most eminent historical grammarian. Late nineteenth- and early twentieth-century grammarians theorized that English came from the Teutonic branch of the Indo-European family of languages, not the Italic branch. They believed that modern English should not be taught the same way as Latin grammar. Unlike Latin, English has word order and is somewhat free of inflections.

Structural grammar has its roots in the work of Leonard Bloomfield (1933), C. C. Fries (1940), Bernard Bloch and George L. Trager (1942), Henry L. Smith (1951), and others. Whereas traditionalists stress the written language, structuralists stress the spoken language. Much attention is given to describing what happens in a sentence, not to prescribing what ought to happen. To the structuralists, grammar is a description of usage, not a prescription of "correctness" or "incorrectness." Emphasis is placed on description of form class words (nouns, verbs, adjectives, and adverbs), structure words (determiners, auxiliaries, pronouns, conjunctions, prepositions, etc.), and sentence patterns (noun–verb, noun–verb–adverb, noun–verb–object, noun–verb–predicate noun, noun–verb–predicate adjective, etc.).

Transformational grammar is the newest way of describing our language. The major contributor to this system is Noam Chomsky of the Massachusetts Institute of Technology. The term "transformational grammar" was introduced in 1957 when he published *Syntactic Structures* (Hague). Transformational grammar focuses on the sentence as the basic unit of communication rather than on the word as in traditional grammar. This grammar is based on the assumption that most English sentences are transformations (variations) of a few basic sentence patterns that are simple, active voice statements (e.g., noun–verb, noun–verb–object, noun–verb–predicate adjective). The grammar of these basic sentence patterns can be expressed in the following formula: Sentence = Determiner + Noun + Number + Tense + (Modal) + (Have + en) + (Be + ing) + Main Verb. The grammatical elements in parentheses may or may not appear in a basic sentence pattern. The only two that must appear are "tense" and "main verb." The elements will always appear in the order given in the formula with the first element denoting the tense of the verb. Only two tenses, past and present, need to be taught. The long conjugations taught by the traditionalists are unnecessary.

Transformationalists demonstrate how mature, complex sentences can be produced from the basic sentence patterns through the processes of substitution, modification, and coordination (e.g., Jerry is tired. Sue is tired. Jerry and Sue are tired.). Through observation of these changes, students are led to develop their own definitions and make discoveries about the structure of their language.

The operation of transformational rules upon basic sentence patterns presumably accounts for all the complicated sentences that are found in our language, especially in mature prose. Because of this claim, transformational grammar is a very powerful grammar.

Several advantages can be derived from the eclectic approach used in this book:

1. Teachers and students do not have to abandon previous training completely. They do not have to unlearn traditional grammar or any other approach. The different approaches can and should supplement and complement one another. New approaches are usually well received by the learner if he is helped to understand what they are and what he can do with them.

2. Each of the large areas of grammar—morphology and syntax— receives adequate treatment, not a superficial recognition.

3. The organization of the book stresses inductive reasoning. The student is led to discover for himself many characteristics of parts of speech, sentence patterns, noun phrases, verb phrases, and transformations.

4. The material is presented clearly and specifically through rules, definitions, examples, and activities. The activities are practical, varied, and short so that one or more may be completed and discussed during a single class period. The content of many of the activities is related to social studies so as to have broader educational appeal to students and teachers.

The content of this book can be studied in two sequences. The first chapter may be used as an introduction to the smallest meaningful units of the English sentence—the parts of speech—or it may follow the second chapter, which introduces the larger, more complete units of English syntax—the sentence patterns. The remaining chapters should be studied in their numbered sequence. Each chapter is summarized to provide the reader with a sense of completeness and achievement.

It is my belief that a knowledge of the "new" English grammar does contribute to the student's competence in speaking and writing when the instruction is focused on the sentence and the ways in which the sentence is changed through various transformations. In addition, such a knowledge of grammar aids the student of literature in clarifying meanings. *The New English Grammar* is designed to help the reader reach these goals.

Acknowledgements

I wish to thank a few of the many people who assisted me in the preparation of the manuscript.

First, I thank six English majors at Memphis State University for their tireless efforts in doing research on structural and transformational grammars during the early stages of the project: Don Presley, Shirley Scott, Dianne Logan, Mary Hysmith, Martha Hysmith, and Patricia Harder.

Second, I thank Professor Juanita Williamson, LeMoyne College, Memphis, and Professor June Morris, Memphis State University, for their technical assistance.

Third, I thank eight English teachers in the Memphis City Schools for evaluating and testing samples of the manuscript: Martha Flowers, Hamilton High School; Adrian McClaren, White Station High School; Martha Dargie, Wooddale Junior High School; Eva Miller, Messick High School; Gladys Ellis, Treadwell High School; Mary Hartsfield, Snowden Junior High School; Olivia Perry, Manassas High School; and Fannie M. Delk, Carver High School.

And last, I thank my wife, Julia, and two sons, Stanley and Sidney, for their understanding and encouragement.

CHARLES LAMAR THOMPSON

Chapter 1
Parts of Speech

The parts of speech in English can be classified into two groups:

1. *Form class words:* nouns, verbs, adjectives, and adverbs.
2. *Structure words:* determiners, pronouns, auxiliaries, prepositions, qualifiers, and conjunctions.

Form class words can change their form through inflection (e.g., from a singular noun to a plural noun) and derivation (e.g., from a verb to a noun). The meaning of form class words is primarily lexical. That is, their meanings are carried by themselves.

Structure words, unlike the form class words, have little lexical meaning. Their meaning is primarily grammatical—it depends upon the form class word that the structure word signals or points out.

To determine the part of speech of a form class word, we can ask three major questions:

1. What is the form of the word?
2. What is the position of the word in the sentence?
3. What is the structure word that signals the form class word?

1

NOUNS

Form of Nouns

Nouns are form class words because we can add -*s* to most nouns to make them plural. The -*s* added to a noun to make it plural is called an **inflectional suffix**. This inflectional suffix is characteristic of nouns and is a clue to recognizing a noun. An inflectional suffix changes the *form* of the word but doesn't change the *class* of the word.

Observe the following:

Singular	Plural
table	tables
vegetable	vegetables
box	boxes

A **derivational suffix**, on the other hand, helps a form class word change from one word class to another word class, e.g., from a verb to a noun, from an adjective to an adverb, etc. Here are some examples of nouns made from verbs and adjectives:

-er: travel*er*, writ*er*
-ion: invent*ion*, percept*ion*
-ness: hard*ness*, kind*ness*
-ity: pur*ity*, san*ity*
-ment: treat*ment*, pay*ment*

Derivational suffixes used to make form class words are called **bound morphemes.** These suffixes cannot function alone—they are bound to other forms. Morphemes are either *free* or *bound*. **Free morphemes** are *words* because they can stand alone.

ACTIVITY 1*

Are the following words nouns? Try forming the plural by adding the inflectional suffix -*s* to the words.

1.	art	6.	slowly
2.	boy	7.	book
3.	donkey	8.	tree
4.	house	9.	small
5.	baseball	10.	bank

*Answers to all of the activities follow Chapter 5.

ACTIVITY 2

Make nouns out of the following words.

1.	defer	6.	cruel
2.	judge	7.	sick
3.	drive	8.	resent
4.	electric	9.	inflect
5.	amaze	10.	holy

Position of Nouns

Nouns can occupy three positions in a sentence: before a verb, after a verb, and after a preposition.

Consider this sentence:

> The *storm* destroyed our *home* in *April.*

The noun *storm* precedes the verb and functions as the subject. The noun *home* follows the verb and serves as the direct object. The noun *April* follows the preposition and functions as the object of the preposition.

Look at this sentence:

> Morris, my *brother,* gave *me* a *watch.*

The noun *brother* precedes the verb and functions as the appositive. The pronoun *me* follows the verb and functions as the indirect object. The noun *watch* follows the verb and functions as the direct object.

Observe this sentence:

> Patricia is my oldest *sister.*

The noun *sister* follows the verb and functions as the predicate noun.

ACTIVITY 3

Copy the following sentences and underline the words that occupy noun positions.

1. Michelangelo Buonarroti was born near Florence, Italy, in 1475.
2. Michelangelo painted scenes from the Bible on the ceiling of the Sistine Chapel in Rome.
3. One of these scenes is the "Creation of Man."

4. Some people consider Michelangelo the ideal Renaissance Man.
5. Michelangelo died in Rome in 1564.
6. Georges Seurat was born in France in 1859.
7. Seurat, a great artist, is famous for his painting technique called *pointillisme*.
8. His pictures consist of thousands of precise dots that give his scenes an originality.
9. One of his most famous paintings, *Sunday on the Grand Jatte*, is at the Art Institute in Chicago.
10. The people and animals in *Sunday on the Grand Jatte* look like monuments.

DETERMINERS: NOUN SIGNALS

Nouns can be recognized by certain structure words that precede them. Look at this sentence:

> *The* election of *a* representative is *a* responsibility
> of *the* people.

The word *the* is a determiner which signals that the nouns *election* and *people* are to follow. The other determiner in the sentence is the word *a* which signals that the nouns *representative* and *responsibility* are to follow. Both *the* and *a* are called **regular determiners.**

Regular determiners include the following:

articles (the, a, an, each, some)
demonstrative pronouns (this, that, these, and those)
possessive pronouns (my, your, his, her, its, our, their)

Regular determiners can be followed by **postdeterminers,** which differ from regular adjectives because they must occur in a fixed order. Postdeterminers include:

ordinals (first, second, third, fourth, etc.)
cardinals (one, two, three, four, etc.)
comparatives and superlatives (more, most, less, least, etc.)

Predeterminers can precede regular determiners and postdeterminers. Predeterminers are separated from the regular determiner by the word *of.*

some (of)   several (of)   any (of)

Consider the following sentence:

All of the seven boys were chosen.

In this sentence, *all of* is the predeterminer, *the* is the regular determiner, and *seven* is the postdeterminer.

PRONOUNS: NOUN SUBSTITUTES

We have already learned that demonstrative and possessive pronouns are structure words that function as determiners. In addition to acting as determiners, pronouns can also function as nouns when they occupy noun positions:

She wrote a short story.
A short story was written by *her*.
Yours is being painted purple.
Larry gave *himself* a shot.
Who invited the man from Florida?

The pronoun *she* in the first sentence is in the **nominative case.** Other pronouns that can be used in the nominative case are:

Singular	Plural
I	we
you	you
he, she, it	they

The pronoun *her* in the second sentence is in the objective case. Other pronouns that are used in the objective case are:

Singular	Plural
me	us
you	you
her, him, it	them

Possessive pronouns can also function as nouns when they occupy noun positions. Some of these pronouns are:

Singular	Plural
mine	ours
yours	yours
his, hers	theirs

Another group of pronouns can function as nouns. These pronouns are called **reflexives** and **intensifiers:**

Singular	*Plural*
myself	ourselves
yourself	yourselves
himself, herself, itself	themselves

Still another group of pronouns that can function as nouns are the following:

who, whoever, whom, whomever, whose
which, whichever
what, whatever

When pronouns function as nouns, they do not have structure words that signal them.

Mother placed *her* apron on the table. (pronoun as structure word)
We gave *her* the apron. (pronoun as noun)

ACTIVITY 4

Copy the following sentences. Place N over each word that occupies a noun position. Underline all determiners that signal the nouns.

1. Archimedes was a leader of scientific exploration during the Hellenistic era.
2. As early as the third century B.C., Archimedes developed the scientific law of specific gravity.
3. Euclid, a contemporary of Archimedes, founded such a complete system of geometry that it remains in use today.
4. Eratosthenes, a mathematical astronomer, was able to determine the size of the earth by the use of scientific principles.
5. Eratosthenes was the first geographer to plot a map indicating lines of latitude and longitude.
6. He is recognized as the founder of scientific geography.
7. Aristotle and his followers were the leaders in the areas of botany and zoology.
8. From their extensive studies of anatomy, these early scientists were able to conclude that the brain was the center of the nervous system.
9. Aristotle also developed the profound theory that the earth was round.

10. A great university in Alexandria attracted many scholars, including Euclid and Hemophilus.

ACTIVITY 5

Identify the pronouns that function as nouns in the following sentences.

1. Meriwether Lewis and William Clark, who led the Lewis and Clark Expedition, were born in Virginia.
2. William Clark was the younger brother of George Rogers Clark, who won fame in the American Revolution.
3. Their expedition took them up the Missouri River, to the Columbia River, and to the Pacific Ocean.
4. They made canoes to carry them through the Snake and Columbia rivers.
5. The journals that they kept contain accounts of their adventures.
6. Lewis and Clark knew themselves much better after their expedition.
7. What fame they got was well deserved.

PREPOSITIONS: NOUN SIGNALS

Another group of structure words which signal that nouns are to follow is prepositions. Prepositions relate nouns to other nouns, verbs, and adverbs in the sentence.

Subject	Verb	Preposition	Determiner	Noun
He	is	in	the	building.
Tommy	slept	during	a	storm.
Faye	worked	for	her	father.

Some of the most frequently used prepositions are:

on	to	before	beyond	over
out	from	about	like	into
in	during	off	between	after
of	inside	up	under	at
with	by	down	around	above

A preposition and its noun object are called a **prepositional phrase.** A prepositional phrase can function in a sentence as an adjective or adverb.

ACTIVITY 6

Identify the prepositions and the nouns they signal in the following sentences.

Example: My study of Greek mythology was interesting.

1. The *Illiad* and the *Odyssey* are the two greatest epics in Greek literature.
2. Homer wrote both of these epics.
3. Some modern critics believe that the *Illiad* and the *Odyssey* were not written by any one poet but were the composite products of many poets.
4. The *Illiad* is the tragic story of Achilles and an episode in the war between the Greeks and the Trojans.
5. The *Odyssey* is a tragic comedy about the wanderer Odysseus.
6. On his travels, Odysseus battles the Cyclops, loses his ship and his crew, and finally, disguised as a beggar, returns to his own palace.
7. Greek drama developed from the singing and dancing at the festivals honoring Dionysus.
8. Lyrics were also popular in Greek literature.
9. Originally, lyrics were poems sung by individuals to a lyre or to a flute.
10. One of the more famous poets in Greek literature was the woman Sappho.

VERBS

Form of Verbs

Verbs are form class words because we can add the inflectional suffix -*s* to third person, present tense verbs to make them singular:

listen*s*, play*s*, take*s*, employ*s*, follow*s*

We can also add the inflectional suffix -*ing* to verbs to form the present participle:

serv*ing*, swimm*ing*, snow*ing*, see*ing*, scar*ing*

Verbs can also be recognized by the inflectional suffix -*ed* that is added to most verbs to form the past tense:

word*ed*, hop*ed*, plann*ed*, pitch*ed*, invit*ed*

There are some verbs that form the past tense by changing within, rather than by adding an inflectional suffix:

Present	Past
begin	began
win	won
sit	sat
ride	rode
drink	drank

The most versatile verb in the English language is *be,* which has eight forms. The verb *be* can be used as the main verb or as a structure word. The *position,* rather than the *form,* is the major clue for determining whether *be* is used as a form class word or a structure word.

> The bell *is* in the tower. (form class word)
> The bell *is* ringing. (structure word)

Position of Verbs

The most common position of the verb is following the subject. Observe the verb in the following sentence patterns:

Subject–Verb: Anthony swims.
Subject–Verb–Direct Object: The hunter killed a deer.
Subject–Verb–Predicate Noun: A policeman is my neighbor.
Subject–Verb–Predicate Adjective: Mother is energetic.

Verbals

Not all words that end in *-ing, -en,* or *-ed* function as verbs. Some words in a sentence may have these inflected endings but function as other form class words. Such words are called **verbals.** Consider these sentences:

> *Seeing* is *believing.*
> The car *passing* is John's.

Seeing in the first sentence functions as a noun subject. *Believing* functions as a predicate noun. In the second sentence *passing* functions as an adjective.

Consider this sentence:

> The athlete wanted to win the medal.

The infinitive *to win* (to + verb) in this sentence completes the verb *wanted* and functions as a noun object, or direct object.

ACTIVITY 7

Copy the following sentences and underline and label the *-ing*, *-ed*, and infinitive (*to* + *verb*) forms of the verbs that function as other parts of speech.

Example: For the Indians, <u>fishing</u> (N) was a major way of <u>getting</u> (N) food.

1. Weaving, hunting, and wild seed gathering were some of the interests of the Basket Maker Indians.
2. The beginnings of the Basket Maker Indians are obscure.
3. Flattening the back of the heads of the Pueblo Indians was achieved by fastening the child to a hard cradleboard.
4. The roofs of the cliff houses of the Pueblo Indians were constructed to carry great weights by laying heavy beams, covering these beams with mats, and then laying on these mats a coat of adobe six to eight inches thick.
5. No single reason is given to explain the moving away of these Indians.
6. The Pueblo Indians knew how to choose farmlands containing rich soil.
7. By performing masked dances, Pueblo youths were initiated into manhood.
9. Men and women, initiated into societies whose main purpose was curing, built outdoor shrines.
9. House clusters belonging to these Indians are evident in Utah, Arizona, and New Mexico.

AUXILIARIES: VERB SIGNALS

Just as nouns have determiners that signal them, verbs may have structure words that precede and signal them. Words that signal verbs are called **auxiliaries.**

> am, is, are, was, were, be, being, been
> have, has, had
> will, would, shall, should
> may, might, can, could
> ought, dare
> do, did, done

Auxiliary verbs can signal *uninflected verbs:*

The soldier will *shoot* to kill.
He can *golf* well.

They can also signal inflected verbs with *-ing, -en,* or *-ed* endings:

Aaron is *sleeping.*
The lake has *frozen* over.
The lady was *helped* across the street.
Margaret will have *forgotten* by now.

Verb Tenses

Main verbs and auxiliaries have two tenses, *present* and *past.* When a main verb is signaled by an auxiliary, the tense of the auxiliary determines the tense of the main verb. If there is more than one auxiliary, the first one will denote the tense.

His office is *closed* on Saturday. (present tense)
His office was *closed* on Saturday. (past tense)
His office will *close* on Saturday. (present tense)
His office will be *closed* on Saturday. (present tense)
His office should be *closed* on Saturday. (past tense)

ACTIVITY 8

Copy the following sentences on your paper and underline the main verbs. If the main verb has an auxiliary, draw an arrow from it to the main verb.

Example: The squirrel has climbed the tree.

1. Lou Gehrig, infielder for the New York Yankees, was elected to the Hall of Fame in 1939.
2. The National Baseball Hall of Fame is located in Cooperstown, New York.
3. Joe DiMaggio of the New York Yankees used a hook slide.
4. Baseball is the national game of the United States.
5. The outfielders in baseball are called right fielder, center fielder, and left fielder.
6. A baseball team is comprised of nine players.
7. If a player leaves the game, he is not permitted to return.

8. The pitcher aims at the "strike zone."
9. Before leagues were started, the players played baseball barehanded.
10. Besides a uniform and glove, the catcher wears a mask, chest protector, and shin guards.

ACTIVITY 9

Copy the following sentences on your paper and underline and label (1) the *verbs*, (2) the *auxiliary verbs* that point to the main verbs, and (3) the *verbals* that function as other parts of speech.

Aux   V   Adv
Example: The inventor is copyrighting to protect his material.

1. Benjamin Franklin invented the Pennsylvania fireplace, which is better known as the Franklin stove.
2. By flying a kite in a thunderstorm, Franklin attempted to prove the identity of lightning and electricity.
3. Franklin spent an hour or two each day in mastering foreign languages and expanding his knowledge.
4. Benjamin Franklin was one of seventeen children.
5. Franklin was granted honorary degrees from Harvard and Yale.
6. Alexander Graham Bell, inventor and physicist, was born in Scotland.
7. Bell is noted for his invention of the telephone.
8. In 1872, Alexander Graham Bell opened a school in Boston for training teachers of deaf-mutes.
9. Another of Bell's inventions is the photophone, an instrument for transmitting sounds in a beam of light.
10. Bell was appointed a regent of the Smithsonian Institution in 1898.

ACTIVITY 10

Copy the following sentences on your paper and identify the nouns, verbs, determiners, auxiliaries, prepositions, and verbals. Use the symbol VER for verbals.

D   N   Aux   V   P   N
Example: The explorers will search for new frontiers.

1. The surrounding islands of Antarctica were discovered in the eighteenth century.

2. The first humans that approached the frozen seas of Antarctica were probably the Polynesians.
3. Captain James Cook and his sailing ships, the *Resolution* and the *Adventure*, approached the continent of Antarctica.
4. After Cook's voyage, mariners began to enter this unknown region.
5. Captain Daniel F. Greene was the first American to approach this area.
6. Sailors in the early nineteenth century made voyages to Antarctica.
7. On an expedition for Russia, Fabian von Bellingshausen was the first person to sight land in this area.
8. A lake that is so salty that the water does not freeze exists in Wright Valley in Antarctica.
9. The only known active volcano in Antarctica is Mt. Erebus.
10. Exploration and research continue today in this vastly unknown area of the world.

ADJECTIVES

Forms of Adjectives

Adjectives, like nouns and verbs, can be identified by their form and position in sentences. Adjectives are form class words because they can change their form through comparison by adding inflectional suffixes:

great	great*er*	great*est*

The inflectional suffixes -*er* and -*est* indicate comparative and superlative degrees of *great*.

Some adjectives that have two or more syllables form their comparative and superlative degrees by having a structure word precede them:

more versatile   more basic   most energetic   most faithful

Some adjectives do not form their comparatives and superlative degrees by adding inflections or small structure words to them. These adjectives are called **irregular adjectives.**

good	better	best
bad	worse	worst
little	less	least

Some uninflected adjectives can be recognized by their endings:

-ly: friendly, lovely   -ary: contrary
-ful: truthful, helpful   -less: painless, hopeless
-ous: gracious, famous   -ive: active, passive
-ish: mannish, Spanish

Some inflected verbs, such as typ*ing* and brok*en*, can function as adjectives if they precede nouns:

The *typing* clerk has a *broken* finger.

ACTIVITY 11

Compare the following adjectives.

Example: *Positive*   *Comparative*   *Superlative*
           capable   more capable   most capable

1. pretty
2. famous
3. lovely
4. selfish
5. bad
6. faithful
7. basic
8. small
9. large
10. impressive

Position of Adjectives

In addition to looking at the form of adjectives to recognize them, we can also observe the positions they usually occupy in a sentence. The most frequently used positions are:

1. adjective before a noun. (the blue jacket)
2. adjective after a verb. (The jacket is blue.)
3. adjective after a noun. (the jacket, blue and gold)

ACTIVITY 12

Using form and position clues, identify the adjectives in the following sentences.

1. The speedboat is usually small and swift in calm water.
2. Sailboats are built to rigid classifications.

3. Large sailboats, roomy and steady, are wholly enjoyable.
4. The canoe, a versatile craft, is popular for fishing.
5. A "scow" is a long, extremely flat boat.
6. A large cruiser has all the accommodations that a home might have.
7. Bigger cruisers are capable of venturing into the ocean.
8. Prams and dinghies are small, light boats that may be towed or taken aboard a yacht.
9. Some classes of sailboats compete in national, international, and regional competition.
10. The construction of small plastic boats began in 1876.

ACTIVITY 13

Identify and label the nouns, verbs, and adjectives in the following sentences.

Example: Military officers train their fighting men.

1. The American Revolution is sometimes called the American War of Independence.
2. In this war the colonies separated themselves from the mother country, England.
3. The American Revolution is significant in history because the colonies succeeded in defeating the parent state.
4. America received powerful aid from France, Spain, and Holland during this war.
5. The American Revolution was fought on land and at sea.
6. John Paul Jones operated from French bases during this war to cruise around the coasts of England.
7. He captured the British ship, the *Serapis*.
8. The American Revolution is considered one of the greatest naval wars in history.
9. The decisive battle of this war came at Yorktown.
10. The surrender of Cornwallis at Yorktown marked the victory of the colonists.

ADVERBS

Form of Adverbs

We are now ready to study the fourth form class word, the adverb. Adverbs are called form class words primarily because they can be changed by adding the derivational suffix -*ly*:

happi*ly*   snug*ly*
slow*ly*   rapid*ly*

Some adverbs can also function as other parts of speech. These adverbs do not change their form. Some of them are:

up	over	here
out	fast	there
near	in	often
still	around	inside
after	while	always

Position of Adverbs

Adverbs can occupy several positions in a sentence.

1. They appear at the beginning of a sentence: *Fortunately,* the road is being repaired.
2. At the end of a sentence: The road is being repaired, *fortunately.*
3. Between a subject and its verb: Mark *certainly* is my friend.
4. Between a main verb and its auxiliary: Maurice will *certainly* mail the package.

Adverbs can modify complete sentences, verbs, adjectives, and other adverbs.

QUALIFIERS: ADJECTIVE AND ADVERB SIGNALS

Qualifiers are structure words that signal adjectives and adverbs. A qualifier immediately precedes the adjective or adverb it modifies.

Adjective qualifier: The concert was *most* unusual.
Adverb qualifier: The audience applauded *most* enthusiastically.

The list of qualifiers can be learned quickly. Here are some that are frequently used:

very	much	least	almost
pretty	more	too	somewhat
fairly	most	so	just
really	less	quite	little

ACTIVITY 14

Identify the adverbs in the following sentences.

1. The exact date of Christopher Columbus' birth is not known.
2. One of Columbus' ships, the *Marigalante*, was officially renamed the *Santa Maria*.
3. Vicente Yáñez Pinzón, the captain of the *Nina*, later became known as one of the finest sailors of the time.
4. After two months of sailing in 1492, Columbus and his men finally reached Guanahani.
5. There Columbus carried the royal banner of Spain.
6. The *Santa Maria* was completely destroyed while Columbus was on the island of Hispaniola.
7. Because of the destruction of this ship, Columbus deliberately left some of his men there.
8. On their return voyage to Spain, Columbus certainly chose a more northerly course.
9. Pinón strongly disapproved this decision.

ACTIVITY 15

Identify and label the nouns, verbs, adjectives, and adverbs in the following sentences.

$$\text{Example:} \quad \overset{N}{\text{Music}} \overset{Adv}{\text{wholly}} \overset{V}{\text{dominated}} \text{Beethoven's} \overset{N}{\text{life.}}$$

1. A very highly regarded musician is Ludwig van Beethoven, who was born in Germany in the eighteenth century.
2. Beethoven studied music too laboriously under the direction of his father.
3. The realization that he was losing his hearing nearly drove the composer to kill himself.
4. It became quite difficult to converse with this musician.
5. In later years all communication was achieved entirely through writing.
6. Biographical material about this composer is partly revealed in Beethoven's letters and notes.
7. Often Beethoven would be overcome by fits of rage that increased with his total deafness.

ACTIVITY 16

Identify and label the determiners, prepositions, auxiliaries, and qualifiers in the sentences in Activity 15.

CONJUNCTIONS

The final group of structure words is the conjunction. The two types of conjunctions are called *coordinating conjunctions* and *subordinating conjunctions.*

The coordinating conjunctions are:

> and, but, or, nor, for, either, neither, so

These conjunctions connect form class words with other words of the same form class:

> nouns with nouns (oranges or pears)
> verbs with verbs (listened and laughed)
> adjectives with adjectives (tall and handsome)
> adverbs with adverbs (slowly but gently)

Coordinating conjunctions also join phrases with phrases and clauses with clauses:

> over the building *and* into the street
> Angelo left, *but* I remained.

Subordinating conjunctions signal noun and adverb clauses:

> She knew *that* (it was raining). (noun clause)
> I finished *before* (you did). (adverb clause)

The following words function as subordinating conjunctions when they signal noun clauses and adverb clauses only:

if	although	that	whereas
till	when	until	in order that
while	where	unless	as if
since	before	because	provided that
after	why	whenever	how
as	than	whether	so that

ACTIVITY 17

Identify the coordinating and subordinating conjunctions in the following sentences.

> Example: He and his friend sailed after Cook died.

1. In the sixteenth century, the Dutch and the English sent explorers to the Arctic so that trade routes could be found.
2. While these two countries were trying to find trade routes,

Peter the Great of Russia sent out the Great Northern Expedition during the eighteenth century.
3. Although Vitus Bering, a Dane in the Russian navy, sailed through the Bering Strait from the south, he failed to notice the significance of this feat.
4. In 1778, Captain James Cook, an explorer for Great Britain, sailed through the Bering Strait and landed at Cape Schmidt.
5. In 1610, Henry Hudson and his crew on the *Discovery* sailed into Hudson Bay.
6. There was a mutiny on the *Discovery*, and Hudson and some of his crew were left to die in a small boat while the mutineers sailed for home on the *Discovery*.
7. Sir John Franklin, an English explorer, and his crew were sent by England in 1845 to find the Northwest Passage.
8. Franklin and his crew never returned, and the loss of this expedition resulted in a twelve-year search for survivors.
9. It was believed that Franklin and his men abandoned their ships and eventually died.
10. Because of their explorations, Robert McClure and Sir John Franklin are credited with the discovery of the Northwest Passage.

ACTIVITY 18:   CHAPTER REVIEW

Identify and label the nouns (*N*), verbs (*V*), adjectives (*Adj*), adverbs (*Adv*), determiners (*D*), prepositions (*P*), auxiliaries (*Aux*), qualifiers (*Q*), and coordinating (*C*) and subordinating (*S*) conjunctions in the following passage.

The recognition of parts of speech is merely part of the process of recognizing larger structures. We take in phrases and utterances as wholes, and seldom bother to analyze them, even unconsciously, into their parts. Just as we recognize a friend by the whole pattern of his appearance, posture, and movement, without analyzing his face into features and his body into individual limbs, so we comprehend a linguistic structure as an organized whole, into which the various parts fit harmoniously. It is only when we wish to describe our friend, or when he shows up with a broken nose or a new kind of haircut, that we become conscious of his individual features. Similarly, it is only when we wish to describe a linguistic structure, or when there is something out of place or novel about it, that we analyze it into its component parts of speech.[1]

[1]W. Nelson Francis, *The Structure of American English* (New York: The Ronald Press Company, 1958), p. 290. Reprinted with the permission of The Ronald Press Company.

Chapter 2
Basic Sentence Patterns

When we look at a sample of English writing, it may appear at first that all of the sentences are different. However, if we look closely at the way the sentences pattern, we may see that they are very similar.

The following passage has thirteen sentences. Read it slowly, observing the words that function as subjects, verbs, and objects of verbs.

South of the United States border lies the beautiful land of Mexico. It is very different from its northern neighbor. Most of its people are mixed Spanish and Indian or pure Indian. They speak the Spanish language. Many of them also speak an Indian language.

Mexico was a civilized Indian country long before Columbus discovered America. Its name comes from the Aztec god of war, Mexitili. In 1521 a handful of Spanish adventurers conquered Mexico. Few of them brought wives and children. They married the Indian women. The children of those marriages formed a new race in the New World. From the Spaniards the Indians took the Spanish language and the Roman Catholic religion. They kept many of the customs of their Indian ancestors—the arts, the handicrafts, the beautiful fiestas, even certain forms of government and land ownership.[1]

[1]*Compton's Pictured Encyclopaedia and Fact-Index*, Volume 14, p. 239. Copyright, 1968. Reprinted with the permission of the F. E. Compton Company, Division of Encyclopaedia Britannica, Inc.

Now that you have read the preceding passage observe how the thirteen sentences pattern:

1. lies–land . . . . Verb–Subject
2. It–is–different . . . . . . Subject–Be Verb–Predicate Adjective
3. Most–are–Spanish
   and Indian . . . . Subject–Be Verb–Predicate Noun
4. They–speak–
   language . . . . Subject–Verb–Direct Object
5. Many–speak–
   language . . . . Subject–Verb–Direct Object
6. Mexico–was–country   Subject–Be Verb–Predicate Noun
7. name–comes . . . . Subject–Verb–(Adverb)
8. Handful–conquered–
   Mexico . . . . Subject–Verb–Direct Object
9. Few–brought–wives
   and children. . . . . . . Subject–Verb–Direct Object
10. They–married–
    women . . . . Subject–Verb–Direct Object
11. Children–formed–
    race . . . . Subject–Verb–Direct Object
12. Indians–took–lan-
    guage and religion . . Subject–Verb–Direct Object
13. They–kept–many . . . Subject–Verb–Direct Object

The five most frequently used sentence patterns in English are:

   I. Subject–Verb–(Adverb)
  II. Subject–Be Verb–Adverb
 III. Subject–Verb–Direct Object
  IV. Subject–Verb–Predicate Noun
        Be
   V. Subject–Verb–Predicate Adjective
        Be

Although *be* is the most common linking verb in modern English, many others are in common use. Verb in Patterns IV and V
                                                                    Be
indicates that the verb may take a form of *be* or some other verb such as *remain* or *become*.

We can see that the sample passage contains all of the basic sentence patterns except Pattern II. Perhaps you have noted that all of the sentences in the sample passage are made up of two

parts: a *noun phrase* and a *verb phrase*. Whenever a noun phrase
and a verb phrase are joined to make a simple statement or declarative sentence in the active voice, a basic sentence pattern results.
More complicated sentences are produced by changing, rearranging, or even substituting different structures in the basic sentence.
Some of the sentence patterns in the sample passage have been
expanded to include modifiers, appositives, compounds, etc.

SENTENCE PATTERN I:
SUBJECT–VERB–(ADVERB)

Pattern I is the most simple pattern. In this pattern the verb is
intransitive. It does not transfer any action to a receiver. The only
action with which the sentence is concerned is that performed by
the subject. Sentence 7 in the sample passage is a good example of
a Pattern I sentence.

Subject   Verb   (Adverb)
name   comes

ACTIVITY 1

1. Write five Pattern I sentences, using subject and verb.
2. Write five Pattern I sentences, using subject, verb, and
   adverb.

SENTENCE PATTERN II:
SUBJECT–BE VERB–ADVERB

The second sentence pattern includes a subject, a *be* verb (such
as is, are, was, were, and been), and an adverb following the *be*
verb to complete the meaning of the sentence. Because the sample
passage does not include a Pattern II sentence, the following sentences are given to illustrate this pattern:

Mexicans are here.
The fiesta will be tomorrow.

ACTIVITY 2

1. Write five Pattern II sentences, using subject, any form of
   the verb *be,* and an adverb of place.
2. Write five Pattern II sentences, using subject, any form of
   the verb *be,* and an adverb of time.

SENTENCE PATTERN III:
SUBJECT–VERB–DIRECT OBJECT

Sentence Pattern III includes two nouns, a noun and a pronoun, or two pronouns. The first noun or pronoun is used as the subject and the second noun or pronoun is used as the direct object. When a pronoun is used as the direct object it takes the objective form (me, us, him, her, them, whom, whomever). A direct object receives the action of the verb as performed by the first noun or pronoun.

Father took *us* to Mexico.
They left *whom* in Mexico?

In this pattern the verb is called *transitive* and serves to pass action on to a receiver or direct object. Sentences 4, 5, 8, 9, 10, 11, 12, and 13 in the sample passage illustrate Pattern III.

4. They speak the Spanish language.
10. They married the Indian women.

ACTIVITY 3

1. Write five Pattern III sentences, using a noun as receiver of the action.
2. Write five Pattern III sentences, using a pronoun as the subject of the verb.
3. Write five Pattern III sentences, using a pronoun as the receiver of the action.

SENTENCE PATTERN IV:
SUBJECT–<u>VERB</u>–PREDICATE NOUN
BE

In Pattern IV the subject is followed by a *be* verb, a *become* verb, or a *remain* verb. In this pattern the subject and the noun or pronoun that follows the verb stand for the same person, place, or thing.

There are two sentences in the sample passage that illustrate Pattern IV.

3. Most of its people are mixed Spanish and Indian or pure Indian.
6. Mexico was a civilized Indian country long before Columbus discovered America.

Here are some other examples of Pattern IV sentences:

>Most become citizens.
>The Mexicans remained friends.

ACTIVITY 4

1. Write five Pattern IV sentences, using any form of the verbs *become* and *remain*.
2. Write five Pattern IV sentences, using any form of the verb *be*.

SENTENCE PATTERN V: SUBJECT–VERB–PREDICATE ADJECTIVE BE

The fifth sentence pattern is made up of a subject, a *be* verb, a *remain* verb, a *become* verb, or a *sense* verb, and a predicate adjective that follows the verb and describes the subject. Sentence 2 in the sample passage is an example of this pattern:

>2. It is very different from its northern neighbor.

Some other examples are:

>Mexicans seem interested.
>The peppers taste hot.
>The peppers remain hot.

ACTIVITY 5

1. Write five Pattern V sentences, using any form of the *be* verb.
2. Write five Pattern V sentences, using any form of *become, remain, taste, look,* and *seem*.

SUMMARY

From our study of the basic sentence patterns, we have discovered that each of the five patterns has a subject and an active voice verb, and that the subject always precedes the verb. Although the subject remains stationary for each pattern, the predicate changes for each pattern. We have also noted that each sentence pattern is made up of a *noun phrase* and a *verb phrase*, generally called the subject and the predicate.

Basic Sentence Patterns

Patterns	Noun Phrase	Verb Phrase
I. Subject–Verb–(Adverb)	Its name	comes from the Aztec god.
II. Subject–Be Verb–Adverb	Mexicans	are here.
III. Subject–Verb–Direct Object	They	speak the language.
IV. Subject–<u>Verb</u>–Predicate Be Noun	Mexico Most	was the country. become citizens.
V. Subject–<u>Verb</u>–Predicate Be Adjective	It It	is very different. seems different.

Chapter 3
The Noun Phrase

Our study of the basic sentence patterns revealed that a sentence can be divided into a *noun phrase* and a *verb phrase*. It is the purpose of this chapter to examine very closely the grammatical elements that make up the noun phrase.

A noun phrase may contain a *single* word or a *group* of words.

Joseph, I, books, toys
the child, all of the children,
most of the time

The essential elements in a noun phrase are *determiner* (D), *noun* (N), and *number* (N^0). Most often a noun phrase is defined in these linguistic symbols:

$$NP \longrightarrow D + N + N^0$$

Each of these essential elements will be discussed in this chapter. You should remember that each of the basic sentence patterns has a subject noun phrase and that Patterns III and IV have a noun phrase in their verb phrase. (They speak the language. Mexico was the country.)

26

DETERMINERS

You recall that we defined a **determiner** as a structure word that signals a noun. There are three kinds of determiners: *regular determiners, predeterminers,* and *postdeterminers.*

Regular Determiners

This group of determiners includes *articles, demonstratives,* and *possessives.*

Articles may be defined as *definite* or *nondefinite:*

$$\text{Articles} \longrightarrow \left\{ \begin{array}{l} \text{Definite} \\ \text{Nondefinite} \end{array} \right\}$$

The word *the* is the only definite article. The nondefinite article may be *a, an, some,* or *null* $\varnothing$. The null article means that no article exists. Proper nouns and personal pronouns always take the null determiner.

> $\varnothing$ They are my friends.
> $\varnothing$ Sidney is my second son.
> $\varnothing$ You call ($\varnothing$) Stanley.

Consider the articles in the following noun phrases:

> *The* blue stones are valuable. (Definite)
> Stones are valuable. (Null)
> *Some* stones are valuable. (Nondefinite)
> *A* blue stone is valuable. (Nondefinite)

The demonstratives are *this, that, these,* and *those.*

> That material was left by mistake.

Possessives are regular determiners that show ownership: *my, our, your, his, her, its, their.*

> John is swimming in *his* pool.

Activity 1

Copy the following sentences on your paper. Underline the subject noun phrase and indicate whether the determiner is definite or nondefinite. Use $\varnothing$ to indicate a nondefinite null article.

Example: <u>Herbert Hoover</u> had reason to be concerned. $\varnothing$

1. The economy was weakened in the Great Depression.
2. Few people believed it would affect the entire nation.
3. Thousands lost their jobs.
4. The stock market crashed in 1929.
5. The crash was one of the causes of the Great Depression.
6. Fortunes were wiped out.
7. Herbert Hoover was president at this time.
8. Some felt there was no reason to be afraid.
9. Factories closed and banks went out of operation.
10. Many families lived in shacks.

ACTIVITY 2

Copy the following sentences on your paper. Underline and label the articles (A), demonstratives (D), and possessives (P).

              A   P

  Example: All of <u>the</u> men have gone to <u>their</u> homes in

             A

          (∅)New York.

1. Daniel bought a pumpkin.
2. Illinois is a large state.
3. He drank his coffee.
4. Each house burned to the ground.
5. Patricia sold that china vase.
6. She wrote those song poems.
7. My sons whispered.
8. Its color is green.

Postdeterminers

Postdeterminers are small structure words that follow regular determiners. Postdeterminers include *ordinals, cardinals, comparatives,* and *superlatives.*

Ordinals	Cardinals	Comparatives and Superlatives
first	one	more
second	two	most
third	three	less
last, next	several	least

Postdeterminers must always appear in a fixed sequence when used with adjectives, unlike a sequence of adjectives appearing before the noun they modify.

the *first* good month
those *three* tall men
many *more* green tickets

These postdeterminers can also be used together, but they must always appear in this order: ordinal–cardinal–comparative or superlative.

the *first thirty* dollars
the *final sixty* days
the *three most* beautiful paintings

Predeterminers

Predeterminers are small structure words that precede both regular determiners and postdeterminers.

Some of the twenty players.
Several of our twenty players.

Predeterminers include most of the regular determiners and the postdeterminers. The predeterminers are usually separated from the regular determiners by the structure word *of.*

ACTIVITY 3

Copy the following sentences on your paper. Underline and label the predeterminers and postdeterminers found in the sentences.

Example: <u>Many of</u> the <u>more</u> suitable topics were approved.
            Pre   Post

(Note that the subject is *topics; many of* and *more* are determiners that signal the noun.)

1. The first of the presidents to be born in a log cabin was Andrew Jackson.
2. Jackson was one of the founders of the Democratic Party.
3. He vetoed more bills than all of the other presidents before him put together.
4. During the first three months Jackson was in the House of Representatives, he made only two speeches.
5. Some of his militiamen gave him the name "Old Hickory."
6. Many of Jackson's friends wanted him to be president.
7. Among the first things Jackson did when elected president was to begin a program of reform.
8. Many more reforms were in effect before long.

NOUNS

Common nouns can be classified in a variety of ways, but the most logical procedure is to divide them into two groups: *count nouns* and *mass nouns*.

Count Nouns

Count nouns are common nouns that can be counted. Count nouns may be concrete or abstract.

house, tree, truth, virtue, idea, crowd

Count nouns can form plurals and take determiners. A helpful clue in determining whether a noun is a count noun or not is to ask the question, *"How many _____ are there?"* If the question can be asked of the noun, the noun is a count noun. For example:

Soldiers built the bridges.
How many _____ are there?
(soldiers)
(bridges)

Mass Nouns

Mass nouns are not countable. They are not thought of as singular or plural. Usually they represent a quantity of something. For example:

blood, loneliness, furniture

To determine whether a noun is a mass noun ask the question, *"How much _____ is there?"* If the question can be asked of the noun, the noun is a mass noun.

Knowledge is power.
How much _____ is there?
(knowledge)

Nouns can be expressed as *count* or *mass:*

$$\text{Noun} \longrightarrow \begin{cases} \text{Count} \\ \text{Mass} \end{cases}$$

ACTIVITY 4

Tell whether each of the nouns that follow is a count noun or a mass noun.

1. boy	11. hat	21. money
2. meat	12. wheat	22. tea
3. coat	13. rain	23. grace
4. movie	14. mush	24. fowl
5. shoe	15. furniture	25. food
6. gravity	16. horse	26. desk
7. cheese	17. cook	27. light
8. cup	18. nutmeg	28. blood
9. milk	19. ice	29. book
10. cloud	20. butter	30. water

ACTIVITY 5

Identify the common nouns in the following sentences and label them *C* for count and *M* for mass.

1. Integrity was one of George Washington's characteristics.
2. Arithmetic was his favorite subject.
3. He gave up his dream of being a sailor.
4. The occupation he decided on was surveying.
5. The surveying expedition took him to the West.
6. The money he earned enabled him to support himself.
7. Washington became a messenger and warned the British to leave the Ohio Valley.
8. Snow covered the ground.
9. Washington led the first American army.
10. He would not accept any pay for his services.
11. Discouragement came often.
12. Many soldiers enlisted only to collect bonuses offered by Congress.
13. Washington's troops lacked supplies throughout the war.
14. Clothing was scarce.
15. They repeatedly ran out of meat.
16. Many had no shoes.
17. The war was finally won.

Animate Nouns

Count nouns can be divided into animate and inanimate nouns. *Animate nouns* are count nouns that can be used as the subject of verbs like *sleep* and *rest* when such words are used in a literal sense. Thus, one way to find out whether a noun is animate or not is to see if it can be used as the subject of such intransitive verbs.

The girls *sleep.*

Two lions *rest.*

Inanimate Nouns

Count nouns that cannot be used as subjects of the verbs *sleep* and *rest* in a literal sense are **inanimate.**

The book *sleeps.*

My window will *rest* today.

Count nouns can be either animate or inanimate. They cannot be both at the same time. This is indicated as follows:

$$\text{Count Noun} \longrightarrow \left\{ \begin{array}{l} \text{Animate} \\ \text{Inanimate} \end{array} \right\}$$

ACTIVITY 6

Make a list of all the nouns you can think of that can be used as the subject of *sleep* and another list of those that cannot be used as the subject of *sleep.* Remember to distinguish between literal and figurative meanings of the verbs.

Human and Nonhuman Nouns

Animate nouns can be divided into *human* and *nonhuman* nouns. This is expressed as follows:

$$\text{Animate Noun} \longrightarrow \left\{ \begin{array}{l} \text{Human} \\ \text{Nonhuman} \end{array} \right\}$$

When the pronoun *who* can be substituted for the noun in the noun phrase, the noun is said to be **human.** Otherwise, the noun should be considered **nonhuman.**

The *boy* put on his sweater.

Who put on his sweater?

ACTIVITY 7

Copy the following sentences on your paper. Tell whether the italicized nouns are animate or inanimate. If they are animate, tell whether they are human or nonhuman. Use A for animate, I for inanimate, H for human, and N for nonhuman.

1. Young Lyndon Johnson was an excellent *student.*
2. His *parents* urged him to go to college.

3. *Money* was a problem.
4. His first *success* came in politics at college.
5. His *wife* is Claudia Taylor.
6. A *nurse* gave Claudia the nickname "Lady Bird" when Claudia was two years old.
7. The *assassination* of President Kennedy made Mr. Johnson president.
8. The former president owns a large *ranch* in Texas.
9. He has many Hereford *cattle*.
10. The *war* in Vietnam was his chief problem.

NUMBER OF NOUNS

Nouns are either *singular* or *plural*. Nouns that mean one of anything have **singular number.** Nouns that mean more than one have **plural number.** Only count nouns have both singular and plural number.

Singular	*Plural*
army	armies
child	children
Johnson	Johnsons

Mass nouns have only singular number. When these nouns mean more than one, they do not function as mass nouns but as count nouns.

Blood is dripping. (*Blood* is a mass noun in this sentence.)
Crowds bother me. (*Crowds* is a count noun in this sentence.)

A helpful aid in determining whether a noun has singular or plural number is to test the noun in the following frame:

1. _____ is.
2. _____ are.

When *pronouns* function as nouns, they are a kind of noun.

I gave *her* a picture.
She gave *me* one, too.

ACTIVITY 8
Identify the nouns (including pronouns) in the following sentences and tell whether they are *singular* or *plural*.

1. The first president to live in the White House was John Adams.
2. Adams was also one of the signers of the Declaration of Independence.
3. During Adams' term as president, Eli Whitney introduced the system of interchangeable parts.
4. The first woolen mills began operating during Adams' term.
5. Abigal Adams was one of the most informed women of the day.
6. She wrote letters to Adams when he was away.
7. Her letters provide wonderful pictures of colonial life.
8. The Stamp Act angered Adams.
9. He wrote resolutions against the Stamp Act.
10. Finally Britain repealed the Stamp Act.
11. He led the colonists in the fight against other British colonial policies too.
12. The British tea tax enraged Adams and other colonials.
13. One night a band of patriots dumped large quantities of tea into Boston Harbor.
14. Adams called the colonists' action "the most magnificent movement of all."

ACTIVITY 9

Here is a list of nouns. Indicate whether they are count nouns or mass nouns and whether they are singular or plural. Use C for count, M for mass, sing. for singular, and plur. for plural.

1. apprentice	11. interests
2. electricity	12. oil
3. women	13. printer
4. program	14. honors
5. intelligence	15. education
6. scientists	16. cooperation
7. member	17. question
8. patience	18. proposal
9. work	19. colonies
10. inventions	20. tact

ACTIVITY 10: CHAPTER REVIEW

Applying what you have learned about nouns in this chapter, copy the following sentences on your paper and underline the

common nouns. Tell whether they are count (C) or mass (M),
animate (A) or inanimate (I), human (H) or nonhuman (N),
and whether the nouns are singular (sing.) or plural (plur.).

Example: The <u>soldier</u> won many <u>honors.</u>

```
            C                      C
            |                      |
            A                      I
            |                      |
            H                     plur.
            |
          sing.
```

1. My friend is intelligent.
2. Franklin tamed lightning.
3. Vacations cost money.
4. Oil will calm a rough sea.
5. The farmers grew the vegetables.

Chapter 4
The Verb Phrase

Our study of the basic sentence patterns has revealed that each sentence pattern consists of grammatical elements that form a base for thousands of sentences. All of the sentences of our language are either basic sentence patterns or are derived from the basic sentence patterns. The simple, active voice sentences can be divided into two parts: the noun phrase (NP) and the verb phrase (VP). The NP generally functions as the subject; the VP functions as the predicate. (Remember that there can also be a noun phrase in the predicate.) This chapter will study the VP. It must be kept in mind that the VP is written differently for each pattern while the subject NP remains the same. It is the VP that differentiates the sentence patterns.

A set of rules has been established by some linguists concerning the structures of VP's. The first rule that we are concerned with is the general rule which says that a sentence contains a NP and a VP. It is written:

$$S \longrightarrow NP + VP$$

In the sentence "Its name comes from the Aztec god," "Its name" is the NP and "comes from the Aztec god" is the VP.

Basic Sentence Patterns

Patterns	Noun Phrase	Verb Phrase
I. Subject–Verb–(Adverb)	Its name	comes from the Aztec god.
II. Subject–Be Verb–Adverb	Mexicans	are here.
III. Subject–Verb–Direct Object	They	speak the language.
IV. Subject–Verb–Predicate Be Noun	Mexico	was the country.
	Most	become citizens.
V. Subject–Verb–Predicate Be Adjective	It	is very different.
	It	seems different.

ACTIVITY 1

Copy the following NP's and add VP's to make English sentences. Write the complete sentence on your paper, putting a vertical line between the NP and the VP.

Example: The man on the bus | gave Joe a newspaper.

1. My favorite novel
2. Margie
3. Large yellow crayons
4. An elephant
5. The theater
6. A three-pound bass
7. The beach boys
8. Some astronauts
9. He
10. Colonel Jackson

ACTIVITY 2

Take each of the sentences you completed in Activity 1 and cross out all the words and phrases that you think are nonessential. Eliminate everything you can and still have a grammatical sentence. Identify each sentence according to pattern.

A three-pound bass is a beautiful fish.
A bass is a fish. (Pattern IV)

There is a definite order that words must follow in the VP of simple, active voice sentences. All verbs change in orderly ways. Every verb takes a definite form and has one or more auxiliaries. To show this we rewrite VP as *auxiliary* plus the *verb*. Expressed in linguistic symbols this is:

$$VP \longrightarrow Aux + Verb$$

An example of this would be:

$$VP \longrightarrow may + follow$$

Any English verb, in contrast to highly inflected languages such as Latin and Greek, must be in either *present* tense or *past* tense. We must use a combination of auxiliary and main verb to form both tenses in English.

THE AUXILIARY

There are two major types of auxiliaries in English:

$$Aux \longrightarrow Aux_1 (Aux_2)$$

Aux_1 always represents tense. Sometimes it may have a modal.

He *goes*. (Main verbs always have tense attached as Aux_1.)
He *will* go. (The modal *will* is Aux_1 and indicates present tense.)

Aux_2 contains *have* and the *-en* form of the verb, or *be* and the *-ing* form of the verb, or both.

They *have* stol*en* a car.
She *has* help*ed* me.
Jim *had* brough*t* the man.
Mary *is* typ*ing*.
They *are* leav*ing*.
I *was* read*ing* a novel.
They *have* be*en* go*ing* every week.

Thus, Aux can be written as follows:

$$Aux \longrightarrow Tense + (Modal) + (have + en) + (be + ing)$$

Tense

There are two tenses in English, *present* and *past*. Tense is an arbitrary term that applies to auxiliary verbs and main verbs. Tense may be denoted by a modal, a form of *have,* a form of *be,* or a main verb, depending on the choice made.

Tense is one kind of auxiliary that may or may not have a modal and is written in this way:

$$\text{Aux}_1 \longrightarrow \text{Tense} + (\text{Modal})$$

It is important to establish the concept that *tense* and *time* are not identical. *Tense* is an aspect within the language. *Time* is external to language, something in the outside world. Although tense and time are *related,* they are not *identical.* For example, we say, "Treadwell High *debates* East High Thursday" (present tense, but future time signaled by Thursday), and "Larry writes well." (present tense, but past time continuing from the past into the future). To denote present time we have to say, "Larry is writing."

Instead of saying that verbs have *future tense* and *perfect tense* (Larry will write, Larry has written, Larry had written, and Larry will have written), we might consider these to be aspects of the verb as expressed by the auxiliaries. Verbs have at least three principal parts: present, past, and past participle. It is the auxiliaries, such as *will, has, had, will have,* and *will have been,* that indicate what we have traditionally called future and perfect tenses.

ACTIVITY 3

The past tense of some verbs is formed by adding an inflectional morpheme to the root verb. When verbs form their past in this way they are called **regular verbs.** Give the past tense of these verbs.

1. follow	6. organize	11. walk	16. cough
2. direct	7. fade	12. finish	17. start
3. describe	8. invite	13. travel	18. decline
4. approve	9. employ	14. faint	19. obey
5. construct	10. burn	15. miss	20. wait

ACTIVITY 4

In many English verbs the root undergoes a spelling change to form the past tense. These verbs are called ***irregular verbs.*** Give the past tense of these verbs.

1. fly	6. build	11. teach	16. lie
2. say	7. go	12. break	17. fight
3. be	8. drive	13. know	18. blow
4. sit	9. write	14. make	19. pay
5. freeze	10. bring	15. see	20. throw

ACTIVITY 5

The root verb usually functions as the present tense form of the verb. When the root verb is used with *he, she,* or *it,* the morpheme *-s* or *-es* is added to the verb to indicate present tense. What would be the present tense form of the verbs in Activity 4 if *he, she,* or *it* were used?

Modal Auxiliaries

Aux contains four segments, only one of which, *tense,* we have described thus far:

$$\text{Aux} \longrightarrow \underbrace{\text{Tense} + (\text{Modal})}_{\text{Aux}_1} + \underbrace{(\text{have} + \text{en}) + (\text{be} + \text{ing})}_{\text{Aux}_2}$$

Tense is not in parentheses; this indicates that it is required. Each auxiliary must have tense. The other segments are optional; therefore, they are in parentheses. The segments must always appear in the order listed.

The modal is the first optional segment. The principal modal auxiliaries that have present and past tense forms are:

> Present: can, may, will, shall, dare to, need to
> Past: could, might, would, should, dared to, needed to

The modals *ought to* and *must* have only a present tense form.

The modals *shall* and *will* can both be used with first person subjects (*I* and *we*). In fact, *will* is used more frequently in the contracted form *I'll* or *we'll*. There is no difference between "I will play the trumpet" and "I shall play the trumpet." *Will* is used with second (*you*) and third (*he, she, it, they*) person pronouns. *Shall* may be used for emphasis.

> You shall do it.
> He shall do it.

It must be remembered that *tense* is always Aux₁, which may or may not have a modal. A branching tree diagram can illustrate the relationship of tense to modal and main verb.

Soldiers can fight.

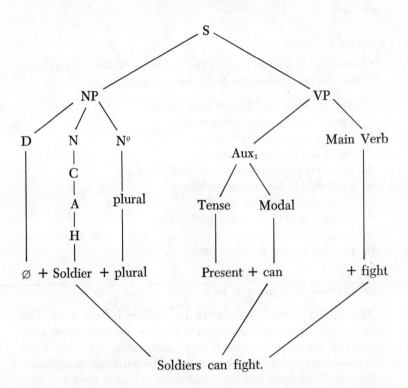

In the diagram above, Aux₁ includes both tense and modal. The modal *can* is a present tense form. The main verb *fight* is a past tense form. Because the tense of Aux₁ always denotes the tense of the main verb, the auxiliary *can* gives us the tense of the verb *fight*.

ACTIVITY 6

Indicate which of the modals listed here will fit into the blank in the following sentence to indicate *present tense*.

The coach _____ signal the quarterback.

1. might	7. can
2. would	8. dares to
3. may	9. must
4. should	10. ought to
5. could	11. shall
6. will	12. needs to

ACTIVITY 7

Identify the modal in each of the following sentences and state whether the *past* or *present tense* form is used.

1. The weather could have been better.
2. I must have money tomorrow.
3. Stanley can play the piano.
4. You may use the telephone.
5. It would require flour, eggs, and sugar.
6. That should be enough lumber.
7. They shall write the senator.
8. Celeste might give the report early.
9. I ought to return the favor.
10. He will answer the question.

The Auxiliary: (have + en)

The second optional segment in the auxiliary is *have + en*. The order of the segments indicates that *have + en* must come after the modal when there is one. If there is no modal, the *have + en* will come after tense. The *en* represents the participle morpheme.

The auxiliary *have* can serve either as the main verb in a sentence or as an auxiliary. The following words are forms of the verb *have* that can be used as an auxiliary:

has, have, had

The auxiliaries *have* and *has* indicate present perfect tense; *had* indicates past perfect tense.

When *have* or one of its other forms is used as an auxiliary, the verb changes its form. This form is called the *en* form. The morpheme *en* is a cover symbol for the past participle form of verbs, including the *ed* morpheme. If the *have* form is used as an auxiliary, the tense is attached to it, and the main verb takes on an *en* form.

The auxiliary *have* is written as follows:

$$(Aux_2) \longrightarrow (have + en)$$

It must be remembered that tense attaches itself to the auxiliary *have*, and the *en* attaches itself to the verb that follows the auxiliary. The parentheses indicate that the auxiliary may be present, but it does not have to be.

ACTIVITY 8

Identify the verbs in the following sentences and then rewrite the sentences by adding a form of *have* as an auxiliary to the verb. If the tense is *present,* use *have* or *has;* use *had* if the tense is *past.*

> *Example:* Carl *entertained* his guests.
> Carl *had entertained* his guests.

1. Herbert walks to school each morning.
2. I punched the time clock.
3. The club chose a leader.
4. Samuel flies a jet.
5. We studied English drama.
6. The soccer player broke his leg.
7. The road glistens in the sunlight.
8. He defeated his opponents.
9. They worry too much about their problems.
10. The policeman gave Lawrence a lecture.

ACTIVITY 9

Copy each of the following sentences on your paper and select the appropriate verb form to match the symbols in parentheses.

> *Example:* Mr. Hunsaker had taken the task seriously.
> (past + have + en + take)

1. Mark _____ his wedding ring.
   (pres + have + en + lose)
2. The student _____ the movie before.
   (past + have + en + see)
3. You _____ a good theme.
   (pres + have + en + write)
4. Dr. McDaniel _____ the lecture.
   (pres + have + en + give)

5. My aunt _____ a nurse.
   (pres + have + en + be)
6. The salesman _____ inside.
   (past + have + en + be)
7. The policeman _____ a suspect.
   (pres + have + en + arrest)
8. Rain _____ the lawn.
   (pres + have + en + cover)
9. Paulette _____ for consideration.
   (past + have + en + ask)
10. Several tourists _____ their cameras.
    (past + have + en + lose)

The Auxiliary: (be + ing)

All of the segments of the auxiliary have been presented except the last one:

Aux ———→ Tense + (Modal) + (have + en) + (be + ing)

Notice that the sequence of four segments contains three that are in parentheses. These elements are optional. The auxiliary must contain *tense*. Tense is not optional. A *modal* or *have* plus a past participle morpheme (*en*) may be included in the auxiliary, or *be* plus the present participle morpheme (*ing*) may be included.

The most complicated verb in the English language is *be*. It is complicated because it has eight forms:

be, is, are, am, was, were, been, being

Each of the forms can be used as an auxiliary. Whenever the auxiliary *be* is present, it consists of a form of *be* plus *ing*, which attaches itself to the main verb. This optional auxiliary can be written as follows:

(Aux$_2$) ———→ (be + ing)

Each of the *be* forms has either past tense or present tense. The past tense forms are:

was, were, been

The present tense forms are:

be, is, are, am, being

A branching diagram can illustrate the relationship of all the segments in the auxiliary.

The soldiers may have been shooting.

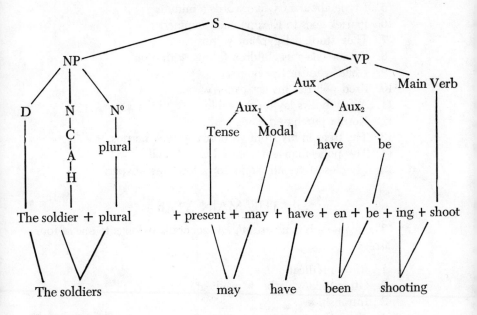

Unlike Latin, Greek, and other highly inflected languages, long conjugations of verbs are not required. One simple formula can be given for all sixteen active tenses in English:

$$VP \longrightarrow \underbrace{Tense + (Modal)}_{Aux_1} +$$

$$\underbrace{(have + en) + (be + ing)}_{Aux_2} + Main\ Verb$$

ACTIVITY 10

Underline the verbs in the following sentences and then rewrite the sentences by adding a form of *be* as an auxiliary to the verb.

Examples: The wind <u>blew</u> the leaves across the yard.
The wind <u>was blowing</u> the leaves across the yard.

1. The librarian sent the professor a letter.
2. My landlady called Mrs. Jetton.
3. The semester draws to an end.
4. Soldiers fight in the jungles.
5. I type about fifty-five words a minute.
6. Patrick goes to Europe each summer.
7. They studied Egyptian culture.
8. Father takes us children fishing with him.
9. I had read for five hours.
10. Fred polishes his car every week.
11. A few books lay on the table.
12. Norma purchased some fruit.
13. The trees in my front yard bear yellow berries.
14. The policeman controlled himself well.
15. My closest friend works for a local newspaper.

THE MAIN VERB

The main verb in a *verb phrase* generally belongs to one of four classes:

1. Be + predicate
2. Other linking verbs + predicate
3. Intransitive
4. Transitive

Some verbs may belong to more than one class. *Be* is always a linking verb, but because of its uniqueness (eight parts) it will be treated separately from the other linking verbs such as *become* and *seem*. For example, consider the sentences: "Judy sings" and "Judy sings ballads." The verb *sings* is intransitive in the former and transitive in the latter. How the verb functions in the sentence determines its classification.

Be + predicate

Every *verb phrase* contains either a *be* verb or another verb. A sentence cannot have both a *be* verb as the main verb and another main verb. To indicate that the main verb is one or the other, the symbol { } is used. Other important points to remember are that a *be* verb always has a predicate and is a linking verb. The predicate may contain a *noun phrase*, an *adjective*, or a *locative adverb* (tells the location of the subject).

$$\text{Verb} \longrightarrow \left\{ \begin{array}{l} \text{Be + pr} \left[\begin{array}{l} \text{NP} \\ \text{Adj.} \\ \text{Loc. Adv.} \end{array} \right] \\ \text{Verb} \end{array} \right\}$$

Be differs from other verbs in having eight distinct forms, not five:

be, being, am, is, are, was, were, been

Be, unlike other verbs, has two past tense forms:

singular (was)
plural (were)

Be also differs from other verbs in having three forms for the present tense:

am, is, are

Sentence Patterns II, IV, and V contain the *be* verb. What constitutes the predicate for each of these patterns?

Activity 11

Identify the noun phrases in each of the following sentences and substitute an equal sign for the *be* form of the verb.

Example: Boxwood is a good hedge.
Boxwood = hedge

1. The winners of the contest were Raymond and Norma.
2. The two senior members are he and Norma.
3. A picnic table was our gift to Miss Anderson.
4. Robert E. Lee was a famous general.
5. Lead is a heavy metal.
6. Carlos will be the judge.
7. Those sailors are my friends.
8. Floyd McCracken is an electrical engineer.
9. He has been the designer for three years.
10. Mr. Claude is our school custodian.

Activity 12

Identify the predicate adjective(s) in each of the following sentences and substitute an equal sign for the *be* form.

Example: Old wine is the best.
wine = best

1. Tommy has been sick for two weeks.
2. Father was unhappy.
3. The steak was expensive.
4. Maps can be very helpful.
5. Jesse is both energetic and imaginative.
6. The dance was dull.
7. The principal is kind, patient, and understanding.
8. They will be loyal to their leader.
9. I am lonesome.
10. Miss Scruggs has always been talkative.

ACTIVITY 13

Identify the locative adverb in each of the following sentences. Remember that **locative** means *location*. This type of adverb completes the sentence by telling us the location of the subject.

1. The postman is outside.
2. Mr. Woody has been there.
3. Friends are nearby.
4. The packages are in the car.
5. Her dog is under the bed.
6. Let's go downstairs.
7. The lining is inside.
8. David is in school.
9. Grandmother's bedroom is upstairs.
10. Stars are in the sky.

Other Linking Verbs + Predicate

Thus far in our analysis of the verb phrase we have discussed auxiliaries and *be*. The verb *be* was separated from all other verbs as follows:

$$\text{Verb} \longrightarrow \left\{ \begin{array}{l} \text{Be} + \text{pr} \left[\begin{array}{l} \text{NP} \\ \text{Adj.} \\ \text{Loc. Adv.} \end{array} \right] \\ \text{Verb} \end{array} \right\}$$

The symbol { } indicates that the main verb must either be a form of *be* or some other main verb. The symbol [ ] indicates that the predicate will include a noun phrase, an adjective, or a locative adverb.

We said that *be* is a linking verb. We are now ready to separate *be* from all other linking verbs. This can be done by using the symbols:

$$\text{Verb} \longrightarrow \left\{ \begin{array}{l} \text{VL} + \text{pr} \begin{bmatrix} \text{NP} \\ \text{Adj.} \\ \text{Loc. Adv.} \end{bmatrix} \\ \\ \text{Verb} \end{array} \right\}$$

Again, we can say that the symbol { } indicates the verb phrase will contain a linking verb plus a predicate or some other main verb. The predicate will contain a *noun phrase*, an *adjective*, or a *locative adverb*. All linking verbs can be followed by adjectives, but not all linking verbs can be followed by noun phrases or locative adverbs. Consider the following general types of linking verbs:

1. *Be, become, appear,* and *remain* verbs that are followed by noun phrases, adjectives, or locative adverbs.
2. *Seem* and other *sense* verbs that are followed by adjectives only.

Sentence Patterns IV and V represent the various forms the linking verbs *become, appear,* and *seem* take:

> Most become citizens.
> They appear happy.
> Margaret seems intelligent.

ACTIVITY 14

Identify the linking verbs in the following sentences. Copy each linking verb on your paper and tell whether it is followed by a *noun phrase*, an *adjective*, or a *locative adverb*.

1. Jonathan seems intelligent.
2. The pickle tasted sour.
3. The team's techniques sound workable.
4. Phoebe's dress became her.
5. The teacher remained in the school.
6. We grew impatient.
7. The audience appeared unhappy.
8. John Baker looks disturbed.
9. I shall remain your friend.
10. Charlie Pendleton became the manager.

11. The flowers turned yellow.
12. Patricia felt strong.
13. The weather has turned cold.
14. The coffee smells strong.
15. Stephen looks ill.

Intransitive Verbs (V_i)

A verb that has *no receiver* of its action is an **intransitive verb.** Intransitive verbs do not have *voice.* That is, the subject is not acted upon, nor is there an object to receive the action of the verb.

Linking verbs are always intransitive, but not all intransitive verbs are linking verbs. The symbol (V_i) is used to denote intransitive verbs that are not linking and that are followed by a *locative adverb,* an *adverb of motion,* or a *manner adverb.*

The following sentences contain intransitive verbs:

$$V_i$$
The children *mumbled.*
$$V_i \text{ (Loc. Adv.)}$$
The children *slept* in the room.
$$V_i \text{ (Adv. of Motion)}$$
The children are *walking* away.
$$V_i \text{ (Manner Adv.)}$$
The children *walked* slowly.

We can symbolize intransitive verbs (V_i) as follows:

$$\text{Verb} \longrightarrow \begin{Bmatrix} V_i \\ \text{Verb} \end{Bmatrix} + \begin{bmatrix} \text{Loc. Adv.} \\ \text{Adv. of Motion} \\ \text{Manner Adv.} \end{bmatrix}$$

The symbol { } indicates that the main verb, other than *be* and other linking verbs, must be intransitive (V_i) verb or a transitive verb (Verb). The symbol [ ] indicates that the intransitive verb may or may not be followed by a *locative adverb,* an *adverb of motion,* or a *manner adverb.*

ACTIVITY 15

Identify the intransitive verbs in the following sentences. Copy each intransitive verb on your paper and tell whether it is followed by a *locative adverb,* an *adverb of motion,* or a *manner adverb.* Some of the intransitive verbs may not have any one of these adverbs.

1. My pet died.
2. Mother works in a jewelry store.
3. Both girls sing well.
4. The birds flew away.
5. My parents live in Illinois.
6. The train moves slowly.
7. Jim and Larry skate dangerously.
8. I stayed at her house.
9. My tooth aches.
10. A student sat on the teacher's desk.
11. The enemy surrendered.
12. Ken reads fast.

Transitive Verbs

We have studied *be* verbs, *VL* verbs, and V_i verbs. There remains one other verb class to be analyzed: *transitive verbs.*

Transitive verbs are always followed by a *noun phrase.* This noun phrase is called a direct object and is identified as Pattern III:

Subject–Verb–Direct Object

Transitive verbs, unlike intransitive verbs, have *voice.* This voice can be either *active* or *passive.* If the verb is in the active voice, the *noun phrase* in the predicate will interchange with the *noun phrase* in the subject:

> They speak the language. (active voice)
> The language was spoken by them. (passive voice)

There is one form of transitive verbs that cannot be made passive. It is called a *mid verb.* The pattern is the same as for the transitive verb:

Subject–Verb–Direct Object

The major difference, however, is that the *mid verb* cannot be made passive. For example, "The fish weighs two pounds" cannot be made passive without changing the meaning of the sentence.

Remember that the transitive verb is always followed by a *noun phrase.* We can symbolize transitive verbs as follows:

$$V \longrightarrow V_t$$

ACTIVITY 16

Copy the following sentences and underline the verbs. Tell whether the verb is *transitive* or *intransitive*. If the verb is *transitive,* indicate if it is *active* or *passive.*

1. The United States Olympic team broke many track records at Helsinki.
2. The mile run was won by Donald Bauer.
3. Uncle Phil's watch cost two hundred dollars.
4. The boy walked slowly.
5. My little nephew weighs thirty pounds.
6. The roast beef and banana cream pie were eaten quickly.
7. Paul smiled sarcastically.
8. Miss Lowe grew some beautiful tomatoes.
9. I must have been taken to the wrong building.
10. Our narcissus plants are growing fast.

SUMMARY

We can visualize the auxiliaries and the four classes of verbs in a branching diagram that looks like this:

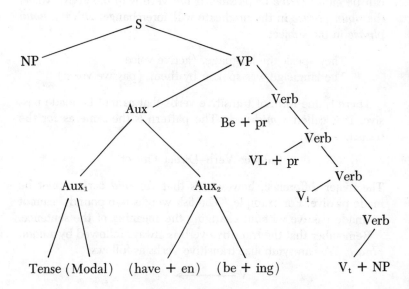

ACTIVITY 17:   CHAPTER SUMMARY

Write kernel sentences for the following strings of symbols.

Example: NP + pres + have + en + V$_t$ + direct object
He has taken the package.

1. NP + past + M + V$_i$
2. NP + past + be + ing + VL + pr
3. NP + pres + M + have + en + V$_t$ + direct object
4. NP + pres + mid verb + direct object
5. NP + past + be + ing + V$_t$ + direct object
   + manner adverb
6. NP + pres + M + have + en + be + ing + V$_i$
   + manner adverb
7. NP + past + have + en + V$_t$ + direct object
8. NP + pres + have + en + be + pr
9. NP + past + V$_i$ + manner adverb
10. NP + pres + M + VL + pr

Chapter 5

Transforming Basic Sentence Patterns

You have observed by now that the basic sentence patterns are elemental structures—simple, declarative, active voice statements —that are formed through the application of phrase structure rules. The essential parts of these basic sentence patterns are the *noun phrase* and the *verb phrase*.

It is not enough that we are able to use these basic sentence patterns in our speaking and writing. We must be able to communicate beyond the elemental level. We must learn how to expand these basic sentence patterns so as to produce more complicated, more mature, more effective sentences in our speaking and writing.

Consider the following:

Alberta went home. Jerry went home. Lillian went home.
Alberta, Jerry, and Lillian went home.

Which of the two examples is more mature, more effective when read aloud? The second example is called a **transform sentence.** A transform sentence is one in which the elements have been changed. A change can come about through the processes of *substitution, modification,* or *coordination.*

54

TRANSFORMING THROUGH SUBSTITUTION

There are many ideas that cannot be expressed by the basic sentence patterns alone. Processes that substitute or replace one word or a group of words with another word or group of words are called *substitution transformations.* These include *question, passive, there,* and *negative* sentences.

Question Transformation

All questions are derived from basic sentence patterns. Questions are usually made by inverting or rearranging the word order of a basic sentence pattern.

> *Pattern V:*   It is very different.
> *Transform:*   Is it very different?

There are two types of question transformations:

1. yes, no
2. who? whom? what? where? when? why? (*wh-* questions)

Yes-No Questions

Any question that can be answered with either "yes" or "no" is a question transformation.

> 1. Mary must work outside. (modal)
>   Must Mary work outside?
> 2. Robert has raised his hand. (have)
>   Has Robert raised his hand?
> 3. The plane is diving. (be)
>   Is the plane diving?

To construct each of the above question transformations, we had to move the auxiliary (modal, have, be) to the frontal position.

Basic sentence patterns do not always have the auxiliaries (modal, have, or be). To form questions from these basic sentence patterns, we add the "do" auxiliary and place it in the frontal position.

> 1. He took the test.
>   Did he take the test?
> 2. Joan plays tennis.
>   Does Joan play tennis?

WH- QUESTIONS

Some questions cannot be answered by a "yes" or "no" response. These questions are introduced by *who, whom, whose, when, where,* or *how.* The *wh-* questions are transformed from *yes-no* questions.

 1. Mexicans are here.
    Are Mexicans here?
    Are who here?
    Who are here?
 2. Frogs sleep in winter.
    Do frogs sleep in winter?
    Do what sleep in winter?
    What sleeps in winter?

ACTIVITY 1

To which of the following sentences can the *yes-no* transformation be applied?

 1. Fashions have symbolized membership in social classes.
 2. They reflect social and economic conditions.
 3. Today fashion is a large industry.
 4. Clothes may express personal taste.
 5. Miniskirts dominated the 1967 fashions.
 6. The fashion image of that year was Twiggy.
 7. She is the youngest of all top models.
 8. The term "in style" suggests conformity.
 9. Fashion predicts social trends.
10. Styles change almost constantly.

ACTIVITY 2

In which of the sentences in Activity 1 is the "do" auxiliary necessary?

ACTIVITY 3

Transform the following sentences into *yes-no* questions, and then into *wh-* questions by substituting *who, what, when,* or *where* for the italicized word.

 1. Inventors are *curious.*
 2. Their *inventions* have satisfied needs.
 3. *Samuel F. B. Morse* developed the telegraph.

4. He also invented a *code*.
5. The *telegraph* transmitted this code.
6. Some *inventors* work together.
7. Many men developed the *television*.
8. *Inventors* have helped the farmers.
9. Benjamin Holt invented the *tractor*.
10. This invention greatly speeds *farming*.

Passive Transformation

The passive transformation is formed from a Pattern III sentence. The *object* of the verb in the active voice sentence becomes the *subject* of the passive transform.

> *Pattern III*:   They speak the *language*.
> *Transform:*   The *language* is spoken by them.

The subject of the pattern sentence functions as the object of the preposition in the passive transform.

ACTIVITY 4

Underline the *transitive* verbs in the following sentences.

1. In 1956 Elvis Presley exposed rhythm and blues to the white Americans.
2. By the late 1950's rock and roll music dominated the country.
3. Chubby Checker made popular the "twist."
4. American singers influenced foreign musicians.
5. In 1964 the Ed Sullivan Show introduced the Beatles.
6. English musical groups led the worldwide scene for the next few years.
7. Many lyrics carry messages to the listeners.
8. Bob Dylan writes songs of protest.
9. National problems provide the lyrics for many songs.
10. Pleas and protests dominate many of the lyrics.

ACTIVITY 5

Apply the passive transformation to the sentences in Activity 4.

ACTIVITY 6

Use the following noun phrases in Pattern III sentences. Next, transform the pattern sentences into passive sentences. Remember

that the function of the noun phrase changes when an active voice
sentence is transformed into a passive voice sentence.

> *Example:* NP₁   NP₂
>   My mother   a cake
> *Pattern III:* My mother baked a cake.
> *Passive transform:* A cake was baked
>   by my mother.

NP₁	NP₂
1. Christopher Columbus	America
2. The British	colonies
3. Indians	the settlers
4. Other countries	settlements
5. The colonies	independence
6. Many men	the Constitution
7. Pioneers	the West
8. The Emancipation Proclamation	the slaves
9. Laborers	unions
10. The Japanese	Pearl Harbor

ACTIVITY 7

Construct passive transforms from the following sentences.

1. An Egyptian named Hannu led the first exploration.
2. His band explored the Land of Punt.
3. The Minoans followed the Egyptians.
4. These explorers used tiny tublike boats.
5. James Cook, an Englishman, explored the South Pacific.
6. Roman soldiers conquered many new lands.
7. The Chinese explored the East.
8. The desire for wealth inspired many expeditions.
9. Queen Isabella of Spain supported Columbus' travels.
10. Astronauts are now exploring outer space.

There Transformation

The *there* transformation is usually produced from Pattern II
sentences. (Mexicans are here.) The process involves the addition
of *there* and the inversion of the noun, *be,* and its auxiliaries.

> *Pattern II:* Mexicans are here.
> *Transform:* There are Mexicans here.

Pattern II: Some Mexicans have been here.
Transform: There have been some Mexicans here.

The word *there* in the transform sentences is a structure word. It is called an **expletive.**

ACTIVITY 8
Apply the *there* transformation to the following statements.

1. Few mountains are in Africa.
2. Submarine mountains are under water.
3. Many mountain ranges are in the United States.
4. Surveyors were measuring the mountain.
5. A dome mountain range is there.
6. A volcanic mountain is in Washington.
7. A climb is beginning.
8. Men are climbing to the peak.
9. A volcano is erupting.
10. Volcanoes are creating islands.

Negative Transformation

The negative transformation, like the question transformation, depends on the tense-bearing word in the verb phrase.

When a *modal*, a *have* auxiliary, or a *be* verb bears the tense, the negative transformation is formed by placing *not* after the *modal, have* auxiliary, or *be* verb.

David must try. David must not try. (modal)
They have gone. They have not gone. (have)
They are here. They are not here. (be)

If the verb is not a *modal*, a *have* auxiliary, or a *be* verb but bears the tense, place *do not* or *does not* before the present tense of the verb and *did not* before the past tense of the verb.

Pattern I: Its name comes from the Aztec god.
Transform: Its name does not come from the Aztec god.

Pattern I: Its name came from the Aztec god.
Transform: Its name did not come from the Aztec god.

ACTIVITY 9
Pick out the tense-bearing word in each verb phrase and tell which negative transformation it requires.

1. Indians lived in the Americas thousands of years before the white settlers came.
2. Indian tribes must have varied widely in their ways of living.
3. Some were warlike, while others were peaceful.
4. Natural resources were discovered by many tribes.
5. The Indians taught white settlers how to grow corn and potatoes.
6. Methods of cooking these crops were also part of their teachings.
7. Words such as *hominy* and *chipmunk* were borrowed from the Indians.
8. Many states have Indian names.
9. Hundreds of cities, rivers, and mountains have Indian names.
10. *Canada* and *Mexico* are both Indian names.

ACTIVITY 10

Construct negative transformations from the following sentences.

1. Family life was an important part of the Indian society.
2. Each member had particular duties to perform.
3. The women cared for the children, cooked, and made the clothes.
4. Their husbands' duties included hunting and working in the field.
5. Small children assisted their mother.
6. Teen-agers were considered men and women.
7. Boys had to prove their bravery by experiencing painful initiations.
8. Marriage partners were chosen by the parents.
9. Ability to work hard was an important factor in their choice.
10. Grandparents, uncles, aunts, cousins, husband, wife, and children lived together.

TRANSFORMING THROUGH MODIFICATION

Our study of the basic sentence patterns revealed that the only modifiers (words restricting the meaning of other words or groups of words) included in them were the adverb and the predicate adjective in the verb phrase. To construct prepositional phrases, infinitives, participles, relative pronouns, relative adverbs, adjectives and adverbs in the noun phrase, and other modifiers, it is important that we know the processes whereby these modifiers transform basic sentence patterns.

Adjective Transformation

Our Pattern V sentence includes Subject–Verb–Predicate Adjective.

The land is very different.

We use Pattern V in producing an adjective transformation. First, expand a Pattern V sentence by including a relative pronoun (*whom, who, that, which*). Then, place the predicate adjective before the noun it modifies.

> *Pattern V (base):*   The land is very different.
> *Step 1:*   The land which is very different
> *Step 2:*   The different land

The pattern sentence can also be called a **base** sentence. Not all base sentences are pattern sentences. For example, a base sentence containing an adjective or a prepositional phrase in the subject noun phrase is a transform sentence.

Step 1 can be called an **insert**. The relative pronoun *which* is inserted into the base sentence.

Step 2 is called a **transform** and is produced through a change of the base and the insert.

Our example can read as follows:

> *Base:*   The land is very different.
> *Insert:*   The land which is very different
> *Transform:*   The different land

Activity 11

Transform the following Pattern V sentences into noun phrases with adjective modifiers. Write out the inserts and the transforms.

> *Example:*   Pattern V: Swimmers are graceful.
>   Insert: Swimmers who are graceful
>   Transform: Graceful swimmers

1. Sports are exciting.
2. Many sports are popular.
3. Some baseball is professional.

4. Many sportsmen are skilled.
5. Football is competitive.
6. Wrestling is combative.
7. Some athletes are professional.
8. Some sports are historic.
9. Their development was gradual.
10. These games are Grecian.
11. Basketball is worldwide.

Adverb Transformation

Adverbs that modify nouns are produced from Pattern II sentences by the same process used to produce adjective transformations.

> Pattern II (base):   Mexicans are here.
> Insert: Mexicans who are here
> Transform: Mexicans here

Unlike the adjective, the adverb usually follows the word modified rather than preceding it.

Prepositional Phrase Transformation

The process of producing prepositional phrase transformations is practically the same as the one used for producing adjective and adverb transformations. Pattern II sentences are used for producing many prepositional phrase transformations.

> Base: Mexicans are in here.
> Insert: Mexicans who are in here
> Transform: Mexicans in here

A prepositional phrase transformation that contains the preposition *with* is produced from a Pattern III sentence containing a form of *have*.

> Base: We have our language problems.
> Insert: We who have our language problems
> Transform: We with our language problems

ACTIVITY 12

Transform the following pattern sentences into noun phrases with adverbial modifiers. Write out the inserts and transforms.

Example: Pattern: Some professionals are here.
Insert: Some professionals who are here.
Transform: Some professionals here

1. Sports are everywhere.
2. Some games are inside.
3. A team is outside.
4. All players are here.
5. The equipment was nearby.
6. That game is tomorrow.
7. The games were yesterday.
8. The champion is downstairs.
9. Many amateurs are there.
10. Tennis is everywhere.
11. The tournament is today.

ACTIVITY 13

Use the noun phrases and their adverbs in Activity 12 to make complete sentences.

Example: Sports everywhere draw many people.

ACTIVITY 14

Transform the following bases into noun phrases with prepositional phrase modifiers. Write out the inserts and transforms.

Example: Base: Sailboats are on sale.
Insert: Sailboats which are on sale
Transform: Sailboats on sale

1. Sailboats are on the lake.
2. Some sailing is in competition.
3. The bow is in the front.
4. The stern is in the rear.
5. Some sailboats are built from kits.
6. The keel is under the hull.
7. Sails are on the boat.
8. The spinnaker is for speed.

ACTIVITY 15

Produce transforms from the following inserts and put the transforms into the given bases to form transform sentences.

Example: Base: We saw sails blowing in the breeze.
            Insert: Sails are of many sizes
            Transform: Sails of many sizes.
            Sentence: We saw sails of many sizes
                        blowing in the breeze.

1. *Base*:   Sailing brings enjoyment to many people.
   Insert: Sailing is for fun.
2. *Base*:   Catboats may be used for racing.
   Insert: Catboats have one sail.
3. *Base*:   Large sailboats compete in some races.
   Insert: Some races are on the ocean.
4. *Base*:   Schooners may be used for long journeys.
   Insert: Schooners have living areas.
5. *Base*:   Strong winds cannot tear the sails.
   Insert: The sails are of dacron.
6. *Base*:   These sailboats are called "prams."
   Insert: These sailboats are for beginners.
7. *Base*:   Yawl is the name given to these boats.
   Insert: These boats have many sails.
8. *Base:*   The sailboats were replaced by steamships.
   Insert: The sailboats had strong floors.
9. *Base*:   Professional boat builders construct many sailboats.
   Insert: Many sailboats are for pleasure.

Indirect Object Transformation

Consider the following sentences:

> Dad bought a car for mother.
> Dad bought mother a car.

In the first sentence *car* is the direct object of the verb, and
mother is the object of the preposition. In the second sentence *car*
is the direct object of the verb, and *mother* is the indirect object.
The indirect object transformation requires that the object of the
preposition in a Pattern III sentence be placed before the direct
object and that the preposition be deleted.

ACTIVITY 16

Transform the following Pattern III sentences into indirect
object transformations.

1. Jane typed a letter for me.
2. Father took the prescription to the pharmacist.
3. I threw the ball to the coach.
4. Leon will take the books to Judd.
5. The mailman handed the package to the child.
6. The boys won honors for themselves.
7. Hubert wrote a poem for his sweetheart.
8. Robert shipped the fruit to his brother.
9. The teacher gave the book to me.
10. He left money for you.

Objective Complement Transformation

Sometimes the direct object in a Pattern III sentence will need a word or phrase to complete the transitive verb. This word or phrase is called the *objective complement.*

D.O.   obj. C.

We elected *Timothy reporter.*

D.O.   Obj. C.

He urged the *crowd* to *leave.*

D.O.   Obj. C.

The men required *him* to *enroll.*

ACTIVITY 17

Construct an objective complement transform sentence from each pair of base and insert sentences.

Example: Base: The mother named the boy.
          Insert: The boy was Moses.
          Transform sentence: The mother named the boy
                             Moses.

1. *Base:*   They named the city.
   Insert: The city was New Orleans.
2. *Base:*   Melvin chose his partner.
   Insert: The partner was John.
3. *Base:*   He found the job.
   Insert: The job was rewarding.
4. *Base:*   The students wanted Larry.
   Insert: Larry was the captain.
5. *Base:*   Women made the movie.
   Insert: The movie was successful.

Infinitive Phrase of Purpose Transformation

An infinitive phrase of purpose can modify an element in a base sentence. The process requires a change in an insert sentence.

> *Base:* George went to the library.
> *Insert:* George planned his trip.
> *Transform:* in order for George to plan his trip
> *Sentence:* George went to the library to plan for his trip.

Notice that the verb *planned* in the insert sentence has been replaced with *to plan* in the transform. The morpheme *-ed* has been dropped, leaving only the base form of the verb. All sentences can contain an infinitive phrase of purpose by placing *in order for (to)* before the sentence (transform) and making the other necessary transformations (sentence).

ACTIVITY 18

Transform each insert into an infinitive phrase of purpose and add it to the predicate of the base sentence.

> *Example:* Base: The game was delayed a week.
> Insert: We must learn the rules.
> Transform sentence: The game was delayed a
>   week in order for us to
>   learn the rules.

1. *Base:* Father had to buy a ticket.
   Insert: He rented a boat.
2. *Base:* Inexpensive boats have been built.
   Insert: Millions of people enjoy pleasure boating.
3. *Base:* Permits were issued.
   Insert: Some motorboats are used for racing.
4. *Base:* Clearance had to be obtained.
   Insert: Hydroplanes skim over the water.
5. *Base:* Residence must be established.
   Insert: A boater buys a license.

Participial Phrase Transformation

Consider the following sentences:

> Our *swimming* companion drowned.
> The man *swimming in the lake* screamed.

Swimming is called a **participle,** which is a verb form occupying an adjectival position and modifying a noun. *Swimming in the lake* is a *participial phrase.*

Swimming in the lake is derived by deleting the subject and the *be* verb:

> *Base:* He is swimming in the lake.
>
> *Transform:* swimming in the lake

Whenever a participial phrase includes *-en* or *-ed,* the phrase is transformed from a Pattern III sentence. The *-en* or *-ed* participial phrase generally is transformed from the passive transformation by the deletion of the relative and *be.*

> *Pattern III (base):* I signed the paper.
>
> *Passive transform (insert):* which was taken by the doctor.
>
> *Transform sentence:* I signed the paper taken by the doctor.

Activity 19

Copy the following sentences and underline all of the participial phrases.

1. The horses pulling the parade wagon are Clydesdales.
2. Morgans, often ridden by policemen, are all descendants of the stallion Justin Morgan.
3. Draft horses used to pull heavy farm equipment are very strong.
4. Many horses living in Asia and Africa are wild.
5. The five main types of modern horses include various breeds developed by man.
6. Horses found on American plains are descendants of Spanish mounts.
7. German zoologists experimenting in crossbreeding "recreated" the "tarpan."
8. This animal, once roaming wild in Europe, died out almost two hundred years ago.
9. The albino, having no pigment in its coat or eyes, is white from birth.
10. Most of the Appaloosas ridden by cowboys are surefooted and sturdy.

ACTIVITY 20

Construct a relative clause insert for each of the following base sentences. Then, construct a participial phrase transform sentence by embedding the insert clause in the base sentence. Underline the participial phrases.

> *Example:* Base: The man is a sailor.
> Insert: who is rowing
> Transform sentence: The man <u>rowing</u> is a sailor.

1. The children are sons of sailors.
2. Those boats are hydroplanes.
3. Balance requires skill.
4. Hydroplanes reach high speeds.
5. The boat belongs to my uncle.
6. Rowboats are different from canoes.
7. People receive enjoyable exercise.
8. Rowboats can be used in shallow water.
9. Luxury yachts can carry many people on an ocean voyage.
10. A person can handle this boat at very high speeds.

Possessive Transformation

The possessive transformation is derived from a Pattern III sentence formed with *have*.

> *Base:* They speak the language.
> *Insert:* John has a language.
> *Transform sentence:* They speak John's language.

You will note that the possessive in the transform replaces the definite article *the* in the base. The insert must contain a form of *have* and an *article*.

ACTIVITY 21

Construct a possessive transform sentence from each pair of base and insert sentences.

1. *Base:* The worshiper is on the mountain.
   Insert: The moon has a worshiper.
2. *Base:* The satellite is the moon.
   Insert: The earth has a satellite.
3. *Base:* The craters are very large.
   Insert: The moon has craters.

4. *Base:*   The atmosphere produces wind and rain.
   Insert: Unlike the moon, the earth has an atmosphere.
5. *Base:*   The moon is not fixed in the heavens.
   Insert: The earth has a moon.
6. *Base:*   The unanswered questions puzzle them.
   Insert: The astronomers have unanswered questions.
7. *Base:*   The flight to the moon was historical.
   Insert: The astronauts had a safe flight.
8. *Base:*   Courage is greatly admired.
   Insert: The astronauts have courage.
9. *Base:*   New prestige is needed.
   Insert: America has new prestige.
10. *Base:*   An excellent director has much responsibility.
    Insert: Our space program has an excellent director.

Relative Pronoun Transformation

The relative pronoun takes the place of the noun phrase in a relative pronoun transformation.

> NP
> *Base:*   *It* seems different.
> *Transform:*   *which* seems different
>
> NP
> *Base:*   The girl bought *a coat.*
> *Transform:*   The coat *that* the girl bought

The relative pronouns that refer to people are *who, whom,* and *that.* Relative pronouns that refer to nonhuman things are *which* and *that.* Relative pronoun transforms are called **relative clauses.**

Appositive (Deletion) Transformation

An **appositive** renames something that precedes it in a sentence and is usually separated from the sentence by commas:

> Rudolph, a reckless driver, failed the road test.

In the above sentence *a reckless driver* is an appositive. It becomes an appositive through this process:

> *Base:*   Rudolph is a reckless driver.
> *Relative transform:*   who is a reckless driver
> *Appositive (deletion) transform:*   a reckless driver

The appositive transformation is derived from a Pattern IV sentence through the relative pronoun transformation and the deletion transformation. The appositive is always a noun and sometimes has modifiers. It always has a relative pronoun and a form of *be*.

ACTIVITY 22

Construct appositive transform sentences from the following pairs of base and insert sentences.

> *Example:* Base: Paul and Cleo live in Los Angeles.
> Insert: Paul and Cleo are my friends.
> Transform: my friends
> Transform sentence: Paul and Cleo, my friends,
> live in Los Angeles.

1. *Base:*   The book is on the table.
   Insert: The book is a novel.
2. *Base:*   Our dog was killed.
   Insert: Our dog was a poodle.
3. *Base:*   Chicago is a convention city.
   Insert: Chicago is the second largest city in the United States.
4. *Base:*   Danville has a textile mill.
   Insert: Danville is a city in Virginia.
5. *Base:*   Father once lived in Atlanta.
   Insert: Atlanta is the industrial city of Georgia.
6. *Base:*   I invited my brothers.
   Insert: My brothers are James, Stephen, and Maurice.
7. *Base:*   Mr. Martin lives on Emerald Street.
   Insert: Mr. Martin was the driver of the car.
8. *Base:*   Tomorrow we leave for the Ozarks.
   Insert: The Ozarks are the nearest mountains to our home.
9. *Base:*   I am Gary Hill.
   Insert: I am the son of an architect.
10. *Base:*   Those two words are similar.
    Insert: The words are *stationary* and *stationery*.

ACTIVITY 23

Transform each insert sentence into a relative pronoun transform and embed the transform in the base sentence to form a transform sentence.

Example: Base: The girl is in the recital.
Insert: The girl plays the piano.
Transform: who plays the piano
Transform sentence: The girl who plays the piano
is in the recital.

1. *Base:* Some fables are very old.
   Insert: They tell us of the power of music.
2. *Base:* Orpheus charmed trees and stones.
   Insert: He was an ancient Greek.
3. *Base:* *Music* means "the art of the Muses."
   Insert: It comes from a Greek word.
4. *Base:* The first songs are those of primitive people.
   Insert: The songs were recorded.
5. *Base:* Beethoven wrote symphonies.
   Insert: He is acclaimed the greatest composer.
6. *Base:* Richard Wagner wrote themes for the orchestra.
   Insert: The themes reveal character traits.
7. *Base:* Jazz is a series of improvisations on a melody.
   Insert: It is a distinct type of music.
8. *Base:* The Psalms were sung responsively.
   Insert: The Psalms are the words of Hebrew songs.

ACTIVITY 24

A. Make clauses containing relative pronouns from these sentences.

1. Horses are dependable friends and servants of man.
2. The horses are winners.
3. Strength and endurance are two characteristics of a horse.
4. Horses are intelligent creatures.
5. Joe is the owner.

B. Transform the relative pronoun clauses in A to appositive transforms.

Relative Adverb Transformation

Relative adverbs—*where, when,* and *why*—introduce relative adverb clauses. These clauses embedded in base sentences produce relative adverb transformations.

Base: Mexicans are working.
Insert: Jim works *here.* Jim works *where.*
Transform sentence: Mexicans are working
  where Jim works.

Base: That was the reason.
Insert: We waited for that reason.
Transform sentence: That was the reason
  why we waited.

Adverbs in inserts are replaced by relative adverbs.

ACTIVITY 25

Transform each insert into a relative adverb clause introduced
by *where, when,* or *why,* and embed the clause in the base sentence to form a transform sentence.

Example: Base: This is the building.
  Insert: Wanda attends school *here.*
  Transform: *where* Wanda attends school
  Transform sentence: This is the building where
    Wanda attends school.

1. *Base:* That was the reason.
   Insert: Brett refused to go for that reason.
2. *Base:* Uncle Bill killed a deer in Georgia.
   Insert: I killed one there.
3. *Base:* Jimmy screamed.
   Insert: The snake appeared.
4. *Base:* I saw the senator.
   Insert: He was here.
5. *Base:* The maid left the room.
   Insert: The children entered the room.
6. *Base:* That was the reason.
   Insert: He played ball for that reason.
7. *Base:* We met at the park.
   Insert: We played ball at the park.
8. *Base:* We went to California.
   Insert: My sister lives there.

ACTIVITY 26

If the following adverbs were in sentences, would they be replaced by *where* or by *when?*

1. instantly	9.	again
2. there	10.	before
3. often	11.	everywhere
4. yesterday	12.	still
5. out	13.	yonder
6. anywhere	14.	tomorrow
7. afterward	15.	at that time
8. up		

Restrictive and Nonrestrictive Modifiers

A modifier may describe a single word or a whole sentence. If the modifier is essential to the meaning of the sentence, it is said to be restrictive. If the modifier is nonessential to the meaning of the sentence, it is said to be nonrestrictive. Nonrestrictive modifiers are set off by commas.

> *Restrictive:* The *yellow* pencil is big.
> The pencil *that* is on the
> table is big.
> *Nonrestrictive:* Helen, *speaking quietly,* gave
> us directions.
> The directions, *which were clear
> and simple,* helped us.

Introductory participial phrases, long adverb clauses, long prepositional phrases, and infinitive phrases are set off by a comma.

> *Wishing for the best,* we waited patiently.
> *Before we do the work,* we need to take the
> clothes to the laundry.

Some introductory modifiers that are set off by commas are essential to the meaning of the sentence:

> *If you accept our conditions,* we'll
> agree to the proposal.

Activity 27

Tell whether the italicized modifiers are restrictive or nonrestrictive. Punctuate the sentences that need punctuating.

1. American Indians *who live in the hot deserts* do not wear much clothing.

2. Eskimos *who are very interesting people* wear much clothing.
3. People *who live in Alaska* wear much clothing.
4. Animals *that live in deserts* are different from animals that live in snow-covered areas.
5. Cockroaches and beetles *which have no backbones* are small insects.
6. Some insects *which have no backbones* have jointed legs.
7. The wart hog *which lives in Africa* is a fierce wild pig.
8. Some wild pigs *which live in Africa* have tusks.
9. The Chinese developed the *magnetic* compass.
10. *Before they do their work* some inventors invest much money.
11. Inventors worked alone *in the eighteenth century.*
12. *Traveling to other lands* the Greeks searched for new ideas.
13. Thomas Edison patented 1,093 inventions *during his long career.*
14. Gabriel D. Farenheit perfected the thermometer *used by doctors.*

TRANSFORMING THROUGH COORDINATION

Transforming basic sentence patterns through coordination involves the linking of two or more basic sentence patterns or sentence elements. The structure words that coordinate these patterns or elements are:

and, but, or, for, nor, either, neither

Consider the following examples of coordination:

Compound sentence
Base (Pattern I):   Courtney went to Florida.
Insert (Pattern I):   Ted stayed at home.
Transform: Courtney went to Florida, but Ted stayed at home.

Compound elements
Base (Pattern I):   Jim went fishing.
Insert (Pattern I):   I went fishing.
Transform: Jim and I went fishing.

The compound elements transform eliminates the elements in the base that are repeated in the insert. As a result, we have a sentence with compound elements, not a compound sentence.

Activity 28

Identify the coordinators in the following compound transforms.
Tell whether they join sentences or elements.
1. The first national park was established to provide a public
   recreational area and to preserve natural wonders.
2. By 1916 the National Park Service was formed, but twelve
   national parks had already been developed.
3. Many visitors camp on the grounds, but others stay in hotels.
4. The federal government supervises all prices and services
   in the parks.
5. Sequoias grow in Sequoia and Kings Canyon National Parks,
   but a hardwood forest covers Isle Royale.
6. Glaciers can be found in Olympic National Park and in
   Mount Rainier National Park.

Activity 29

Combine each of the following pairs of sentences into a transform containing compound elements.

   Example: Pattern: I saw the movie.
              Pattern: He saw the movie.
              Transform: He and I saw the movie.

1. Sports demand physical skill.
   Sports demand enthusiasm.
2. Baseball can be a competitive sport.
   Swimming can be a competitive sport.
3. Sportsmanship includes honesty.
   Sportsmanship includes cooperation.
   Sportsmanship includes respect for others.
4. Persons of all ages enjoy viewing sports.
   Persons of all ages enjoy participating in sports.
5. Wrestling is a combative sport.
   Fencing is a combative sport.
6. Team sports require teamwork.
   Team sports require fast action.

Activity 30

Construct transforms with compound elements from these bases
and inserts.

1. *Base:* Greek literature affected Latin literature.
   Insert: Greek literature affected English literature.
2. *Base:* Greek literary forms grew out of the Aeolian dialect.
   Insert: Greek literary forms grew out of the Dorian dialect.
3. *Base:* Great historians appeared in the Attic Age.
   Insert: Great orators appeared in the Attic Age.
4. *Base:* The Greeks expressed their feelings through their writing.
   Insert: The Greeks expressed their opinions on life through their writing.
5. *Base:* Lysias was a powerful Greek orator.
   Insert: Isocrates was a powerful Greek orator.
6. *Base:* The Alexandrian Age produced famous dramatists.
   Insert: The Alexandrian Age produced important mathematicians.
7. *Base:* Epigrams flourished in the Byzantine Age.
   Insert: Hymns flourished in the Byzantine Age.

ACTIVITY 31

Coordinate the following pairs of sentences. If the sentences are not related and cannot be coordinated, place an *N* beside the number.

1. Inventors make something new.
   Discoverers find something that already exists.
2. Movable type made possible magazines and books.
   Linotype decreased typesetting time.
3. Some inventors have helped battle disease.
   Others have improved farming methods.
4. Galileo invented the thermometer.
   Gabriel Fahrenheit perfected it.
5. Alfred Nobel created dynamite.
   The atomic bomb is a powerful weapon.
6. Steam first powered the tractor.
   Later, gasoline powered it.
7. Cyrus McCormick invented the reaper.
   Edmund W. Quincy developed the corn picker.
8. Inventions contribute to many areas.
   The television was developed after years of research.
9. Air conditioners cool us in summer.
   Electric heaters keep us warm in winter.

SUMMARY

You will want to review the ways of transforming basic sentence patterns. The chart below should aid you in your review.

Basic Sentence Patterns	Type of Transformation	Sentence Transformations
1. Subject–Verb– (Adverb)	Negative	Its name does not come from the Aztec god.
	Compound elements	Jim and I went fishing.
	Compound sentence	Courtney went to Florida, but Ted stayed at home.
II. Subject– Be Verb– Adverb	Yes–no question	Are they here?
	Wh- question	Who are here?
	There	There are Mexicans here.
	Adverb	Mexicans here are farmers.
	Prepositional phrase	Mexicans in here work.
	Participial phrase	The man swimming in the lake screamed.
		The enemy, faced with the odds, surrendered.
III. Subject–Verb– Direct Object	Passive	The language is spoken by them.
	Indirect object	Dad bought Mother a car.
	Objective complement	We elected Tom reporter.
	Infinitive phrase	George went to the library to plan his trip.
	Possessive	They speak John's language.

Basic Sentence Patterns	Type of Transformation	Sentence Transformations
IV. Subject–Verb–Be Predicate Noun	Appositive (deletion)	Rudolph, a reckless driver, is my brother.
	Relative adverb	That was the reason why we waited.
	Negative	
	Yes—no question	Is he John?
V. Subject–Verb–Be Predicate Adjective	Yes-no question	Is it very different?
	Adjective	A different land is Mexico.
	Relative pronoun	The coat that the girl bought is pretty.

Answers for Chapter 1: **Parts of Speech**

Activity 1

1. arts
2. boys
3. donkeys
4. houses
5. baseballs
6. slowly (an adverb)
7. books
8. trees
9. small (an adjective)
10. banks

Activity 2

1. deferment
2. judgment
3. driver
4. electricity
5. amazement
6. cruelty
7. sickness
8. resentment
9. inflection
10. holiness

Activity 3

1. Michelangelo Buonarroti was born near Florence, Italy, in 1475.
2. Michelangelo painted scenes from the Bible on the ceiling of the Sistine Chapel in Rome.
3. One of these scenes is the "Creation of Man."
4. Some people consider Michelangelo the ideal Renaissance Man.
5. Michelangelo died in Rome in 1564.
6. Georges Seurat was born in France in 1859.
7. Seurat, a great artist, is famous for his painting technique called *pointillisme*.
8. His pictures consist of thousands of precise dots that give his scenes an originality.
9. One of his most famous paintings, *Sunday on the Grande Jatte*, is at the Art Institute in Chicago.
10. The people and animals in *Sunday on the Grande Jatte* look like monuments.

Activity 4

1. Archimedes (N) was a leader (N) of scientific exploration (N) during the Hellenistic era (N).

79

2. As early as the third century (N) B.C., Archimides (N) developed the scientific law (N) of specific gravity (N).
3. Euclid (N), a contemporary (N) of Archimedes (N), founded such a complete system (N) of geometry (N) that it (N) remains in use (N) today.
4. Eratosthenes (N), a mathematical astronomer (N), was able to determine the size (N) of the earth (N) by the use (N) of scientific principles (N).
5. Eratosthenes (N) was the first geographer (N) to plot a map (N) indicating lines (N) of latitude (N) and longitude (N).
6. He (N) is recognized as the founder (N) of scientific geography (N).
7. Aristotle (N) and his followers (N) were the leaders (N) in the areas (N) of botany (N) and zoology (N).
8. From their extensive studies (N) of anatomy (N), these early scientists (N) were able to conclude that the brain (N) was the center (N) of the nervous system (N).
9. Aristotle (N) also developed the profound theory (N) that the earth (N) was round.
10. A great university (N) in Alexandria (N) attracted many scholars (N), including Euclid (N) and Hemophilus (N).

ACTIVITY 5

1. who
2. who
3. them
4. they, them
5. they
6. themselves
7. what, they

ACTIVITY 6

1. in (P) literature (N)
2. of (P) epics (N)
3. by (P) poet (N), of (P) poets (N)
4. of (P) Achilles (N) episode (N), in (P) war (N), between (P) Greeks (N), Trojans (N)
5. about (P) wanderer (N), Odysseus (N)
6. on (P) travels (N), as (P) beggar (N), to (P) palace (N)
7. from (P) singing (N) dancing (N), at (P) festivals (N)
8. in (P) literature (N)
9. by (P) individuals (N), to (P) lyre (N), to (P) flute (N)
10. of (P) poets (N), in (P) literature (N)

ACTIVITY 7

1. Weaving (N), hunting (N), and wild seed gathering (N) were some of the interests of the Basket Maker Indians.
2. The beginnings (N) of the Basket Maker Indians are obscure.
3. Flattening (N) the back of the heads of the Pueblo Indians was achieved by fastening (N) the child to a hard cradle-board.
4. The roofs of the cliff houses of the Pueblo Indians were constructed to carry (Adv) great weights by laying (N) heavy beams, covering (N) these beams with mats, and then laying (N) on these mats a coat of adobe six to eight inches thick.
5. No single reason is given to explain (Adv) the moving (N) away of these Indians.
6. The Pueblo Indians knew how to choose (N) farmlands containing (Adj) rich soil.
7. By performing (N) masked dances, Pueblo youths were initiated into manhood.
8. Men and women, initiated (Adj) into societies whose main purpose was curing (N), built outdoor shrines.
9. House clusters belonging (Adj) to these Indians are evident in Utah, Arizona, and New Mexico.

ACTIVITY 8

1. Lou Gehrig, infielder for the New York Yankees, was elected to the Hall of Fame in 1939.
2. The National Baseball Hall of Fame is located in Coopers-town, New York.
3. Joe DiMaggio of the New York Yankees used a hook slide.
4. Baseball is the national game of the United States.
5. The outfielders in baseball are called right fielder, center fielder, and left fielder.
6. A baseball team is comprised of nine players.
7. If a player leaves the game, he is not permitted to return.
8. The pitcher aims at the "strike zone."
9. Before leagues were started, the players played baseball bare-handed.
10. Besides a uniform and glove, the catcher wears a mask, chest protector, and shin guards.

ACTIVITY 9

1. Benjamin Franklin invented (V) the Pennsylvania fireplace, which is (Aux) better known (V) as the Franklin stove.
2. By flying (Adj) a kite in a thunderstorm, Franklin attempted to prove (N) the identity of lightning (N) and electricity.
3. Franklin spent (V) an hour or two each day in mastering (N) foreign languages and expanding (N) his knowledge.
4. Benjamin Franklin was (V) one of seventeen children.
5. Franklin was (Aux) granted (V) honorary degrees from Harvard and Yale.
6. Alexander Graham Bell, inventor and physicist, was (Aux) born (V) in Scotland.
7. Bell is (Aux) noted (V) for his invention of the telephone.
8. In 1872, Alexander Graham Bell opened (V) a school in Boston for training (N) teachers of deaf-mutes.
9. Another of Bell's inventions is (V) the photophone, an instrument for transmitting (N) sounds in a beam of light.
10. Bell was (Aux) appointed (V) a regent of the Smithsonian Institution in 1898.

ACTIVITY 10

1. The (D) surrounding (Ver) islands (N) of (P) Antarctica (N) were (Aux) discovered (V) in (P) the (D) eighteenth (D) century (N).
2. The (D) first (D) humans (N) that approached (V) the (D) frozen (Ver) seas (N) of (P) Antarctica (N) were (V) probably the (D) Polynesians (N).
3. Captain (N) James (N) Cook (N) and his (D) sailing (Ver) ships (N), the (D) *Resolution* (N) and the (D) *Adventure* (N), approached (V) the (D) continent (N) of (P) Antarctica (N).
4. After (P) Cook's (D) voyage (N), mariners (N) began (V) to enter (Ver) this (D) unknown region (N).
5. Captain (N) Daniel (N) F. (N) Greene (N) was (V) the (D) first (D) American (N) to approach (Ver) this (D) area (N).
6. Sailors (N) in (P) the (D) early nineteenth (D) century (N) made (V) voyages (N) to (P) Antarctica (N).
7. On (P) an (D) expedition (N) for (P) Russia (N), Fabian (N) von (N) Bellingshausen (N) was (V) the (D) first (D)

person (N) to sight (Ver) land (N) in (P) this (D) area
(N).

8. A (D) lake (N) that is (V) so salty that the (D) water (N)
does (Aux) not freeze (V) exists (V) in (P) Wright (N)
Valley (N) in (P) Antarctica (N).

9. The (D) only known (Ver) active volcano (N) in (P)
Antarctica (N) is (V) Mt. Erebus (N).

10. Exploration (N) and research (N) continue (V) today in
(P) this (D) vastly unknown area (N) of (P) the (D)
world (N).

ACTIVITY 11

1. pretty	prettier	prettiest
2. famous	more famous	most famous
3. lonely	lonelier	loneliest
4. selfish	more selfish	most selfish
5. bad	worse	worst
6. faithful	more faithful	most faithful
7. basic	more basic	most basic
8. small	smaller	smallest
9. large	larger	largest
10. impressive	more impressive	most impressive

ACTIVITY 12

1. small, swift, calm
2. rigid
3. large, roomy, steady, enjoyable
4. versatile, popular
5. long, flat
6. large
7. bigger
8. small, light
9. national, international, regional
10. small, plastic

ACTIVITY 13

1. The American (Adj) Revolution (N) is sometimes called
(V) the American (Adj) War (N) of Independence (N).

2. In this war (N) the colonies (N) separated (V) themselves
(N) from the mother (Adj) country (N), England (N).

3. The American (Adj) Revolution (N) is (V) significant
(Adj) in history (N) because the colonies (N) succeeded
(V) in defeating (N) the parent (Adj) state (N).

4. America (N) received (V) powerful (Adj) aid (N) from France (N), Spain (N), and Holland (N) during this war (N).

5. The American (Adj) Revolution (N) was fought (V) on land (N) and at sea (N).

6. John (N) Paul (N) Jones (N) operated (V) from French (Adj) bases (N) during this war (N) to cruise around the coasts (N) of England (N).

7. He (N) captured (V) the British (Adj) ship (N), the Serapis (N).

8. The American (Adj) Revolution (N) is considered (V) one of the greatest (Adj) naval (Adj) wars (N) in history (N).

9. The decisive (Adj) battle (N) of this war (N) came (V) at Yorktown (N).

10. The surrender (N) of Cornwallis (N) at Yorktown (N) marked (V) the victory (N) of the colonists (N).

Activity 14

1. not
2. officially
3. later
4. finally
5. there
6. completely
7. deliberately, there
8. certainly
9. strongly

Activity 15

1. A very highly (Adv) regarded (Adj) musician (N) is (V) Ludwig (N) van (N) Beethoven (N), who was born (V) in Germany (N) in the eighteenth century (N).

2. Beethoven (N) studied (V) music (N) too laboriously (Adv) under the direction (N) of his father (N).

3. The realization (N) that he (N) was losing (V) his hearing (N) nearly (Adv) drove (V) the composer (N) to kill himself (N).

4. It (N) became (V) quite difficult (Adj) to converse (Adv) with this musician (N).

5. In later (Adj) years (N) all communication (N) was achieved (V) entirely (Adv) through writing (N).

6. Biographical (Adj) material (N) about this composer (N) is partly (Adv) revealed (V) in Beethoven's letters (N) and notes (N).

7. Often (*Adv*) Beethoven (*N*) would be overcome (*V*) by fits (*N*) of rage (*N*) that increased (*V*) with his total (*Adj*) deafness (*N*).

ACTIVITY 16

1. A (*D*) very (*Q*) highly regarded musician is Ludwig van Beethoven, who was (*Aux*) born in (*P*) Germany in (*P*) the (*D*) eighteenth (*D*) century.
2. Beethoven studied music too (*Q*) laboriously under (*P*) the (*D*) direction of (*P*) his (*D*) father.
3. The (*D*) realization that he was (*Aux*) losing his hearing nearly drove the (*D*) composer to kill himself.
4. It became quite (*Q*) difficult to converse with (*P*) this (*D*) musician.
5. In (*P*) later years all (*D*) communication was (*Aux*) achieved entirely through (*P*) writing.
6. Biographical material about (*P*) this (*D*) composer is (*Aux*) partly revealed in (*P*) Beethoven's (*D*) letters and notes.
7. Often Beethoven would (*Aux*) be (*Aux*) overcome by (*P*) fits of (*P*) rage which increased with (*P*) his (*D*) total deafness.

ACTIVITY 17

1. and (*C*), so that (*S*)
2. while (*S*)
3. although (*S*)
4. and (*C*)
5. and (*C*)
6. and (*C*), and (*C*), while (*S*)
7. and (*C*)
8. and (*C*), and (*C*)
9. that (*S*), and (*C*), and (*C*)
10. because (*S*)

ACTIVITY 18:   CHAPTER REVIEW

The (*D*) recognition (*N*) of (*P*) parts (*N*) of (*P*) speech (*N*) is (*V*) merely (*Adv*) part of (*D*) the (*D*) process (*N*) of (*P*) recognizing (*N*) larger (*Adj*) structures (*N*). We (*N*) take (*V*) in (*Adv*) phrases (*N*) and (*C*) utterances (*N*) as (*P*) wholes (*N*), and (*C*) seldom (*Adv*) bother (*V*) to (*P*) analyze (*V*) them (*N*), even (*Q*) unconsciously (*Adv*), into (*P*) their (*D*) parts (*N*). Just (*Q*) as (*S*) we (*N*) recognize (*V*) a (*D*) friend (*N*) by (*P*) the (*D*) whole (*Adj*) pattern (*N*) of (*P*) his (*D*) appearance (*N*), posture (*N*), and (*C*) movement (*N*), without (*P*) analyzing (*N*) his (*D*) face (*N*) into (*P*) features (*N*) and (*C*) his

(D) body (N) into (P) individual (Adj) limbs (N), so (C) we (N) comprehend (V) a (D) linguistic (Adj) structure (N) as (P) an (D) organized (Adj) whole (N), into (P) which (S) the (D) various (Adj) parts (N) fit (V) harmoniously (Adv). It (N) is (V) only (Q) when (S) we (N) wish (V) to describe (N) our (D) friend (N), or (C) when (S) he (N) shows (V) up (Adv) with (P) a (D) broken (Adj) nose (N) or (C) a (D) new (Adj) kind (N) of (P) haircut (N), that (S) we (N) become (V) conscious (Adj) of (P) his (D) individual (Adj) features (N). Similarly (Adv), it (N) is (V) only (Q) when (S) we (N) wish (V) to describe (N) a (D) linguistic (Adj) structure (N), or (C) when (S) there (Expletive) is (V) something (N) out of place (Adj) or (C) novel (Adj) about (P) it (N), that (S) we (N) analyze (V) it (N) into (P) its (D) component (Adj) parts (N) of (P) speech (N).

Answers* for Chapter 3: **The Noun Phrase**

ACTIVITY 1

1. The economy—definite
2. Few people—nondefinite
3. Thousands—∅
4. The stock market—definite
5. The crash—definite

6. Fortunes—∅
7. Herbert Hoover—∅
8. Some—∅
9. Factories—∅
10. Many families—nondefinite

ACTIVITY 2

1. (∅) (A) Daniel bought a (A) pumpkin.
2. (∅) (A) Illinois is a (A) large state.
3. (∅) (A) He drank his (P) coffee.
4. Each (A) house burned to the (A) ground.
5. (∅) (A) Patricia sold that (D) china vase.
6. (∅) (A) She wrote those (D) song poems.
7. My (P) sons whispered.
8. Its (P) color is green.

*The answers for each of the five activities in Chapter 2 will vary. There are no *correct* answers.

ACTIVITY 3

1. The first of (*Pre*)   5. Some of (*Pre*)
2. one of (*Pre*)   6. Many of (*Pre*)
3. all of (*Pre*)   7. first (*Post*)
4. first three (*Post*)   8. Many (*Pre*), more (*Post*)

ACTIVITY 4

1. C	7. M	13. M	19. M	25. M
2. M	8. C	14. M	20. M	26. C
3. C	9. M	15. M	21. M	27. C
4. C	10. C	16. C	22. M	28. M
5. C	11. C	17. C	23. M	29. C
6. M	12. M	18. M	24. C	30. M

ACTIVITY 5

1. integrity, *M*; character-   9. army, *C*
   istics, *C*   10. pay, *M*; services, *C*
2. arithmetic, *M*; subject, *C*   11. discouragement, *M*
3. dream, *C*; sailor, *C*   12. soldiers, *C*; bonuses, *C*
4. occupation, *C*; surveying,   13. troops, *C*; supplies, *C*; war,
   M   *C*
5. expedition, *C*   14. clothing, *M*
6. money, *M*   15. Meat, *M*
7. messenger, *C*   16. shoes, *C*
8. snow, *M*; ground, *M*   17. war, *C*

ACTIVITY 6

Note: Answers will vary.

ACTIVITY 7

1. A, H   6. A, H
2. A, H   7. I
3. I   8. I
4. I   9. A, H
5. A, H   10. I

ACTIVITY 8

1. president—singular   White House—singular
   John Adams—singular

2. Adams—singular   (*One of* is a predeterminer)
   signers—plural   Declaration of Independence—singular
3. term—singular   president—singular
   Eli Whitney—singlar   system—singular   parts—plural
4. mills—plural   term—singular
5. Abigail Adams—singular   (*one of* is a predeterminer)
   women—plural   day—singular
6. She—singular   letters—plural   Adams—singular
   he—singular
7. letters—plural   pictures—plural   life—singular
8. Stamp Act—singular   Adams—singular
9. He—singular   resolutions—plural   Stamp Act—singular
10. Britain—singular   Stamp Act—singular
11. He—singular   colonists—plural   fight—singular
    policies—plural
12. tax—singular   Adams—singular   colonials—plural
13. night—singular   band—singular   patriots—plural
    quantities—plural   tea—singular
    Boston Harbor—singular
14. Adams—singular   action—singular
    movement—singular

ACTIVITY 9

1. C sing.		11. C plur.	
2. M sing.		12. M sing.	
3. C plur.		13. C plur.	
4. C sing.		14. C plur.	
5. M sing.		15. M sing.	
6. C plur.		16. M sing.	
7. C sing.		17. C sing.	
8. M sing.		18. C sing.	
9. M sing.		19. C plur.	
10. C plur.		20. M sing.	

ACTIVITY 10: CHAPTER REVIEW
1. My friend (*C, A, H, sing.*) is intelligent.
2. Franklin tamed lightning (*M, I, sing.*).
3. Vacations (*C, I, plur.*) cost money (*M, I, sing.*).
4. Oil (*M, I, sing.*) will calm a rough sea (*C, I, sing.*).
5. The farmers (*C, A, H, plur.*) grew the vegetables
   (*C, I, plur.*).

Answers for Chapter 4: **The Verb Phrase**

ACTIVITY 1
Note: Answers will vary.

ACTIVITY 2
Note: Answers will vary.

ACTIVITY 3

1. followed	6. organized	11. walked	16. coughed
2. directed	7. faded	12. finished	17. started
3. described	8. invited	13. traveled	18. declined
4. approved	9. employed	14. fainted	19. obeyed
5. constructed	10. burned	15. missed	20. waited

ACTIVITY 4

1. flew	6. built	11. taught	16. lay
2. said	7. went	12. broke	17. fought
3. was	8. drove	13. knew	18. blew
4. sat	9. wrote	14. made	19. paid
5. froze	10. brought	15. saw	20. threw

ACTIVITY 5

1. flies	6. builds	11. teaches	16. lies
2. says	7. goes	12. breaks	17. fights
3. is	8. drives	13. knows	18. blows
4. sits	9. writes	14. makes	19. pays
5. freezes	10. brings	15. sees	20. throws

ACTIVITY 6
3, 6, 7, 8, 9, 10, 11, 12

ACTIVITY 7

1. could—past	6. should—past
2. must—present	7. shall—present
3. can—present	8. might—past
4. may—present	9. ought to—present
5. would—past	10. will—present

ACTIVITY 8

1. walks—Herbert *has walked* to school each morning.
2. punched—I *had punched* the time clock.
3. chose—The club *had chosen* a leader.
4. flies—Samuel *has flown* a jet.
5. studied—We *had studied* English drama.
6. break—The soccer player *had broken* his leg.
7. glistens—The road *has glistened* in the sunlight.
8. defeated—He *had defeated* his opponents.
9. worry—They *have worried* too much about their problems.
10. gave—The policeman *had given* Lawrence a lecture.

ACTIVITY 9

1. has lost
2. had seen
3. have written
4. has given
5. has been
6. had been
7. have arrested
8. has covered
9. had asked
10. had lost

ACTIVITY 10

Note: Answers will vary. For example:
  1. sent—is sending/was sending (Both are acceptable.)

ACTIVITY 11

1. winners = Raymond and Norma
2. members = he and Norma
3. table = gift
4. Robert E. Lee = general
5. Lead = metal
6. Carlos = judge
7. sailors = friends
8. Floyd McCracken = engineer
9. He = designer
10. Mr. Claude = custodian

ACTIVITY 12

1. Tommy = sick
2. Father = unhappy
3. steak = expensive
4. maps = helpful
5. Jesse = energetic and imaginative
6. dance = dull
7. principal = kind, patient, and understanding
8. They = loyal
9. I = lonesome
10. Miss Scruggs = talkative

Activity 13

1. outside
2. there
3. nearby
4. in the car
5. under the bed
6. downstairs
7. inside
8. in school
9. upstairs
10. in the sky

Activity 14

1. seems—adjective
2. tasted—adjective
3. sound—adjective
4. became—noun phrase
5. remained—locative adverb
6. grew—adjective
7. appeared—adjective
8. looks—adjective
9. remain—noun phrase
10. became—noun phrase
11. turned—adjective
12. felt—adjective
13. turned—adjective
14. smells—adjective
15. looks—adjective

Activity 15

1. died
2. works—locative adverb
3. sing—manner adverb
4. flew—adverb of motion
5. live—locative adverb
6. moves—manner adverb
7. skate—manner adverb
8. stayed—locative adverb
9. aches
10. sat—locative adverb
11. surrendered
12. reads—manner adverb

Activity 16

1. broke—transitive—active voice
2. was won—transitive—passive voice
3. cost—transitive—active voice
4. walked—intransitive
4. walked—intransitive
5. weighs—transitive—active voice
6. were eaten—transitive—passive voice
7. smiled—intransitive
8. grew—transitive—active voice
9. must have been taken—transitive—passive voice
10. are growing—intransitive

Answers for Chapter 5: **Transforming Basic Sentence Patterns**

ACTIVITY 1

1, 3, 4, 6, 7

ACTIVITY 2

2, 5, 8, 9, 10

ACTIVITY 3

1. Are inventors curious?
   Who are inventors?
2. Have their inventions satisfied needs?
   What has satisfied needs?
3. Did Samuel F. B. Morse develop the telegraph?
   Who developed the telegraph?
4. Did he also invent a code?
   What did he also invent?
5. Did the telegraph transmit this code?
   What transmitted this code?
6. Do some inventors work together?
   Who work together?
7. Did many men develop the television?
   What did many men develop?
8. Have inventors helped the farmers?
   Who have helped the farmers?
9. Did Benjamin Holt invent the tractor?
   What did Benjamin Holt invent?
10. Does this invention greatly speed farming?
    What does this invention greatly speed?

ACTIVITY 4

1. exposed
2. dominated
3. made
4. influenced
5. introduced
6. led
7. carry
8. writes
9. provide
10. dominate

ACTIVITY 5 (illustrative answers)

1. In 1956 rhythm and blues was exposed to the white Americans by Elvis Presley.
2. By the late 1950's, the country was dominated by rock and roll music.
3. The "twist" was made popular by Chubby Checker.
4. Foreign musicians were influenced by American singers.
5. In 1964 the Beatles were introduced by the Ed Sullivan Show.
6. For the next few years the world-wide scene was led by English musical groups.
7. Messages to the listeners are carried by many lyrics.
8. Songs of protest are written by Bob Dylan.
9. Lyrics for many songs are provided by national problems.
10. Many of the lyrics are dominated by pleas and protests.

ACTIVITY 6 (illustrative answers)

1. Christopher Columbus discovered America.
   America was discovered by Christopher Columbus.
2. The British ruled the colonies.
   The colonies were ruled by the British.
3. Indians helped the settlers.
   The settlers were helped by Indians.
4. Other countries claimed settlements.
   Settlements were claimed by other countries.
5. The colonies declared independence.
   Independence was declared by the colonies.
6. Many men wrote the Constitution.
   The Constitution was written by many men.
7. Pioneers settled the West.
   The West was settled by the pioneers.
8. The Emancipation Proclamation freed the slaves.
   The slaves were freed by the Emancipation Proclamation.
9. Laborers formed unions.
   Unions were formed by laborers.
10. The Japanese attacked Pearl Harbor.
    Pearl Harbor was attacked by the Japanese.

ACTIVITY 7

1. The first exploration was led by an Egyptian named Hannu.

2. The Land of Punt was explored by his band.
3. The Egyptians were followed by the Minoans.
4. Tiny tublike boats were used by these explorers.
5. The South Pacific was explored by James Cook, an Englishman.
6. Many new lands were conquered by Roman soldiers.
7. The East was explored by the Chinese.
8. Many expeditions were inspired by the desire for wealth.
9. Columbus' travels were supported by Queen Isabella of Spain.
10. Outer space is now being explored by astronauts.

ACTIVITY 8
1. There are few mountains in Africa.
2. There are submarine mountains under water.
3. There are many mountain ranges in the United States.
4. There were surveyors measuring the mountain.
5. There is a dome mountain range there.
6. There is a volcanic mountain in Washington.
7. There is a climb beginning.
8. There are men climbing to the peak.
9. There is a volcano erupting.
10. There are volcanoes creating islands.

ACTIVITY 9
1. lived—do transformation
2. must—do transformation
3. were, were—simple negative transformation
4. were—simple negative transformation
5. taught—do transformation
6. were—simple negative transformation
7. were—simple negative transformation
8. have—do transformation
9. have—do transformation
10. are—simple negative transformation

ACTIVITY 10
1. Family life was not an important part of the Indian society.
2. Each member did not have particular duties to perform.
3. The women did not care for the children, cook, and make the clothes.

4. Their husbands' duties did not include hunting and working in the fields.
5. Small children did not assist their mother.
6. Teen-agers were not considered men and women.
7. Boys did not have to prove their bravery by experiencing painful initiations.
8. Marriage partners were not chosen by the parents.
9. Ability to work hard was not an important factor in their choice.
10. Grandparents, uncles, aunts, cousins, husband, wife, and children did not live together.

ACTIVITY 11 (illustrative answers)
1. *Insert:* Sports that are exciting
   Transform: Exciting sports
2. *Insert:* Many sports that are popular
   Transform: Many popular sports
3. *Insert:* Some baseball which is professional
   Transform: Some professional baseball
4. *Insert:* Many sportsmen who are skilled
   Transform: Many skilled sportsmen
5. *Insert:* Football that is competitive
   Transform: Competitive football
6. *Insert:* Wrestling which is combative
   Transform: Combative wrestling
7. *Insert:* Some athletes who are professional
   Transform: Some professional athletes
8. *Insert:* Some sports that are historic
   Transform: Some historic sports
9. *Insert:* Their development which was gradual
   Transform: Their gradual development
10. *Insert:* These games that are Grecian
   Transform: These Grecian games
11. *Insert:* Basketball which is worldwide
   Transform: Worldwide basketball

ACTIVITY 12 (illustrative answers)
1. *Insert:* Sports that are everywhere
   Transform: Sports everywhere
2. *Insert:* Some games that are inside
   Transform: Some games inside

3. *Insert:*   A team that is outside
   Transform: A team outside
4. *Insert:*   All players who are here
   Transform: All players here
5. *Insert:*   The equipment which was nearby
   Transform: The equipment nearby (*or* the nearby equipment)
6. *Insert:*   That game which is tomorrow
   Transform: That game tomorrow
7. *Insert:*   The games which were yesterday
   Transform: The games yesterday
8. *Insert:*   The champion who is downstairs
   Transform: The champion downstairs
9. *Insert:*   Many amateurs who are there
   Transform: Many amateurs there
10. *Insert:*   Tennis which is everywhere
    Transform: Tennis everywhere
11. *Insert:*   The tournament which is today
    Transform: The tournament today

ACTIVITY 14 (illustrative answers)
1. *Insert:*   Sailboats which are on the lake
   Transform: Sailboats on the lake
2. *Insert:*   Some sailing which is in competition
   Transform: Some sailing in competition
3. *Insert:*   The bow which is in the front
   Transform: The bow in the front
4. *Insert:*   The stern which is in the rear
   Transform: The stern in the rear
5. *Insert:*   Some sailboats which are built from kits
   Transform: Some sailboats built from kits
6. *Insert:*   The keel which is under the hull
   Transform: The keel under the hull
7. *Insert:*   Sails which are on the boat
   Transform: Sails on the boat
8. *Insert:*   The spinnaker which is for speed
   Transform: The spinnaker for speed

ACTIVITY 15 (illustrative answers)
1. *Transform:*   Sailing for fun
   Sentence: Sailing for fun brings enjoyment to many people.

2. *Transform:*   Catboats with one sail
   Sentence: Catboats with one sail may be used for racing.
3. *Transform:*   Some races on the ocean
   Sentence: Large sailboats compete in some races on the ocean.
4. *Transform:*   Schooners with living areas
   Sentence: Schooners with living areas may be used for long journeys.
5. *Transform:*   The sails of dacron
   Sentence: Strong winds cannot tear the sails of dacron.
6. *Transform:*   These sailboats for beginners
   Sentence: These sailboats for beginners are called "prams."
7. *Transform:*   These boats with many sails
   Sentence: Yawl is the name given to these boats with many sails.
8. *Transform:*   The sailboats with strong floors
   Sentence: The sailboats with strong floors were replaced by steamships.
9. *Transform:*   Many sailboats for pleasure
   Sentence: Amateur boat builders construct many sailboats for pleasure.

Activity 16

1. Jane typed me a letter.
2. Father took the pharmacist the prescription.
3. I threw the coach the ball.
4. Leon will take Judd the books.
5. The mailman handed the child the package.
6. The boys won themselves honors.
7. Hubert wrote his sweetheart a poem.
8. Robert shipped his brother the fruit.
9. The teacher gave me the book.
10. He left you money.

Activity 17

1. They named the city New Orleans.
2. Melvin chose John to be his partner.
3. He found the job was rewarding.
4. The students wanted Larry captain.
5. Women made the movie successful.

ACTIVITY 18

1. *Transform sentence:* Father had to buy a ticket in order for him to rent a boat.
2. *Transform sentence:* Inexpensive boats have been built in order for millions of people to enjoy pleasure boating.
3. *Transform sentence:* Permits were issued in order for some motorboats to be used for racing.
4. *Transform sentence:* Clearance had to be obtained in order for the hydroplanes to skim over the water.
5. *Transform sentence:* Residence must be established in order for a boater to buy a license.

ACTIVITY 19

1. pulling the parade wagon
2. ridden by policemen
3. used to pull heavy farm equipment
4. living in Asia and Africa
5. developed by man
6. found on American plains
7. experimenting in crossbreeding
8. roaming wild in Europe
9. having no pigment in its coat or eyes
10. ridden by cowboys

ACTIVITY 20 (illustrative answers)

1. *Insert:* riding in the sailboat
   Transform sentence: The children riding in the sailboat are sons of sailors.
2. *Insert:* reaching high speeds
   Transform sentence: Those boats reaching high speeds are hydroplanes.
3. *Insert:* achieved by a back-and-forth motion
   Transform sentence: Balance achieved by a back-and-forth motion requires skill.
4. *Insert:* used on calm water
   Transform sentence: Hydroplanes used on calm water reach high speeds.

5. Insert: taken aback by the wind
   Transform sentence: The boat taken aback by the wind belongs to my uncle.
6. *Insert*:   propelled by oars
   Transform sentence: Rowboats propelled by oars are different from canoes.
7. *Insert*:   rowing ordinary rowboats
   Transform sentence: People rowing ordinary rowboats receive enjoyable exercise.
8. *Insert*:   converted into motorboats
   Transform sentence: Rowboats converted into motorboats can be used in shallow water.
9. *Insert*:   powered by diesel engines
   Transform sentence: Luxury yachts powered by diesel engines are quite expensive.
10. *Insert*:   skilled in sailing
   Transform sentence: A person skilled in sailing can handle this boat at very high speeds.

ACTIVITY 21

1. *Transform sentence*:   The moon's worshiper is on the mountain.
2. *Transform sentence*:   The earth's satellite is the moon.
3. *Transform sentence*:   The moon's craters are very large.
4. *Transform sentence*:   Unlike the moon, the earth's atmosphere produces wind and rain.
5. *Transform sentence*:   The earth's moon is not fixed in the heavens.
6. *Transform sentence*:   The astronomers' unanswered questions puzzle them.
7. *Transform sentence*:   The astronauts' safe flight to the moon was historical.
8. *Transform sentence*:   The astronauts' courage is greatly admired.
9. *Transform sentence*:   America's new prestige is needed.
10. *Transform sentence*:   Our space program's excellent director has much responsibility.

ACTIVITY 22

1. *Transform*:   a novel
   Transform sentence: The book, a novel, is on the table.

2. *Transform*:   a poodle
   Transform sentence: Our dog, a poodle, was killed.

3. *Transform*:   the second largest city in the United States
   Transform sentence: Chicago, the second largest city in the United States, is a convention city.

4. *Transform*:   a city in Virginia
   Transform sentence: Danville, a city in Virginia, has a textile mill.

5. *Transform*:   the industrial city of Georgia
   Transform sentence: Father once lived in Atlanta, the industrial city of Georgia.

6. *Transform*:   James, Stephen, and Maurice
   Transform sentence: I invited my brothers, James, Stephen, and Maurice.

7. *Transform*:   the driver of the car
   Transform sentence: Mr. Martin, the driver of the car, lives on Emerald Street.

8. *Transform*:   the nearest mountains to our home
   Transform sentence: Tomorrow we leave for the Ozarks, the nearest mountains to our home.

9. *Transform*:   the son of an architect.
   Transform sentence: I am Gary Hill, the son of an architect.

10. *Transform*:   *stationary* and *stationery*
    Transform sentence: Those two words, *stationary* and *stationery*, are similar.

ACTIVITY 23

1. *Transform:*   that tell us of the power of music
   Transform sentence: Some fables that tell us of the power of music are very old.

2. *Transform*:   who was an an ancient Greek
   Transform sentence: Orpheus, who was an ancient Greek, charmed trees and stones.

3. *Transform*:   which comes from a Greek word
   Transform sentence: *Music*, which comes from a Greek word, means "the art of the Muses."

4. *Transform*:   that were recorded
   Transform sentence: The first songs that were recorded are those of primitive people.

5. *Transform*:   who is acclaimed the greatest composer
   Transform sentence: Beethoven, who is acclaimed the greatest composer, wrote symphonies.
6. *Transform*:   that reveal character traits
   Transform sentence: Richard Wagner wrote themes that reveal character traits.
7. *Transform*:   which is a distinct type of music
   Transform sentence: Jazz, which is a distinct type of music, is a series of improvisations on a melody.
8. *Transform*:   which are the words of Hebrew songs
   Transform sentence: The Psalms, which are the words of Hebrew songs, were sung responsively.

ACTIVITY 24

A.
1. which are dependable friends and servants of man
2. that are winners
3. which are two characteristics of a horse
4. which are intelligent creatures
5. who is the owner

B.
1. dependable friends and servants of man
2. winners
3. two characteristics of a horse
4. intelligent creatures
5. the owner

ACTIVITY 25 (illustrative answers)

1. *Transform*:   why Brett refused to go
   Transform sentence: That was the reason why Brett refused to go.
2. *Transform*:   where I killed one
   Transform sentence: Uncle Bill killed a deer in Georgia where I killed one.
3. *Transform*:   when the snake appeared
   Transform sentence: Jimmy screamed when the snake appeared.

4. *Transform*: when he was here
  Transform sentence: I saw the senator when he was here.
5. *Transform*: when the children entered the room
  Transform sentence: The maid left the room when the children entered.
6. *Transform*: why he played ball
  Transform sentence: That was the reason why he played ball.
7. *Transform*: where we played ball
  Transform sentence: We met at the park where we played ball.
8. *Transform*: where my sister lives
  Transform sentence: We went to California where my sister lives.

ACTIVITY 26

1. when	4. when	7. when	10. when	13. where
2. where	5. where	8. where	11. where	14. when
3. when	6. where	9. when	12. when	15. when

ACTIVITY 27

1. Restrictive
2. Nonrestrictive (Eskimos, –people,)
3. Restrictive
4. Restrictive
5. Nonrestrictive (beetles,–backbones,)
6. Restrictive
7. Nonrestrictive (hog, –Africa,)
8. Restrictive
9. Restrictive
10. Nonrestrictive (work,)
11. Restrictive
12. Nonrestrictive (lands,)
13. Restrictive
14. Restrictive

ACTIVITY 28

1. and–elements
2. but–sentences
3. but–sentences
4. and–elements
5. and–elements, but–sentences
6. and–elements

ACTIVITY 29

1. Sports demand physical skill and enthusiasm.
2. Baseball and swimming can be competitive sports.

3. Sportsmanship includes honesty, cooperation, and respect for others.
4. Persons of all ages enjoy viewing and participating in sports.
5. Wrestling and fencing are combative sports.
6. Team sports require teamwork and fast action.

ACTIVITY 30

1. Greek literature affected Latin literature and English literature.
2. Greek literary forms grew out of the Aeolian dialect and the Dorian dialect.
3. Great historians and great orators appeared in the Attic Age.
4. The Greeks expressed their feelings and opinions on life through their writing.
5. Lysias and Isocrates were powerful Greek orators.
6. The Alexandrian Age produced famous dramatists and important mathematicians.
7. Epigrams and hymns flourished in the Byzantine Age.

ACTIVITY 31

1. Inventors make something new, but discoverers find something that already exists.
2. Movable type made possible magazines and books, and linotype decreased typesetting time.
3. Some inventors have helped battle disease, and others have improved farming methods.
4. Galileo invented the thermometer, but Gabriel Fahrenheit perfected it.
5. N
6. Steam first powered the tractor, but gasoline later powered it.
7. Cyrus McCormick invented the reaper, and Edmund W. Quincy developed the corn picker.
8. N
9. Air conditioners cool us in summer, and electric heaters keep us warm in winter.